My Wisdom
That No One Wants

Other Books by Nancy Hopkins Reily

I Am At An Age

Classic Outdoor Color Portraits, A Guide for Photographers

Joseph Imhof, Artist of the Pueblos, with Lucille Enix

Georgia O'Keeffe, A Private Friendship,
Part I, Walking the Sun Prairie Land

Georgia O'Keeffe, A Private Friendship,
Part II, Walking the Abiquiu and Ghost Ranch Land

My Wisdom
That No One Wants

Nancy
Hopkins
Reily

SUNSTONE PRESS
SANTA FE

Sunstone books may be purchased for educational, business, or sales promotional use.
For information please write: Special Markets Department, Sunstone Press,
P.O. Box 2321, Santa Fe, New Mexico 87504-2321.

Library of Congress Cataloging-in-Publication Data

Reily, Nancy Hopkins, 1934-
My wisdom that no one wants / by Nancy Hopkins Reily.
p. cm.
ISBN 978-0-86534-776-2 (alk. paper)
1. Life--Quotations, maxims, etc. 2. Conduct of life--Quotations, maxims, etc.
I. Title.
PN6084.L53R44 2010
818'.602--dc22

2010038668

Softcover: 978-1-63293-296-9

SUNSTONE PRESS

WWW.SUNSTONEPRESS.COM
SUNSTONE PRESS / POST OFFICE BOX 2321 / SANTA FE, NM 87504-2321 /USA
(505) 988-4418 / ORDERS ONLY (800) 243-5644 / FAX (505) 988-1025

Dedicated
To
Women Who Want Wisdom
To Finish First,
At Last.

Contents

Foreword

A few years ago after dining at a Chinese restaurant, I received the usual complimentary fortune cookie. When I opened it, the words I read definitely resonated with me. My fortune said, *If you seek wisdom, go ask your mother*. I knew those words to be true because all my life I have been blessed with a mother who has been my best source of wisdom, my go-to person in any dilemma.

Naturally, as a young girl, I always turned to my mother when I needed help with decisions since I had not acquired all the knowledge and experience I needed to navigate every situation. Then when I became an adolescent, I sometimes found myself rebelling against her wisdom, only to later reluctantly accept it. Then once I became an adult and later a mother myself, I regained my appreciation for her wisdom, seeking it often and passing it on to my own children. I have also gone to her many times for affirmation of decisions I have helped my daughters make and have been comforted by her wisdom.

In short, the simplistic words of my fortune cookie continue to ring true, and I thank you, Mom, for always being there with your wisdom and reassurance, and most of all, for always offering them in the most loving way.

—Donna Carolyn Reily Davis

Preface

Years ago my daughter put a framed poster of short sayings in a garage sale. I asked her if I could have the sayings each in a different color. She agreed. I hung the sayings in my utility room bathroom.

All too often women have to wait in line in public ladies' rest rooms. As I would wait I wished for something attractive to look at instead of the bare walls. I thought it would be fun to have a poster of short sayings on the wall.

My original intent was to publish my words of wisdom with each saying in different colors on a vertical poster for use in those public ladies' rest rooms. That led to my writing a similar horizontal version for the men's latrine. In time, I added more subjects on wisdom which could be hung any where horizontally or vertically.

The whole concept became too much for posters, so here is my wisdom in black and white.

Wisdom is thought of in several ways: as a combination of knowledge and experience to improve a person; as the application of knowledge needed to live a good life; as the judicious and purposeful application of knowledge that society values; and as being different from intelligence. Wisdom does not always increase with age; a wise decision can be made with incomplete knowledge.

Some neuroscientists believe wisdom evolves from a small number of brain regions to form a network. The dorsolateral prefrontal cortex controls emotions, processes ambiguity and acts like a disciplinarian father. The ventromedial prefrontal cortex supplies morality, self-reflection, decision making and acts like a nice, kind mother. The anterior cingulate cortex detects conflicts, makes decisions and acts like an uncle you would go to with difficult times. The limbic striatum is part of the brain's reward system and acts like a friend. As these regions balance they lead to a collection of attributes known as wisdom.

Over a lifetime adults are divided into subgroups: young adults who are apprenticing life, the not so young adults who think they know everything, the thirty somethings who are approaching master craftsmanship in living, the middle-aged contemplating denial, those of a "certain age" as described by the French, and finally the mature adult who has lived through many critical times.

As a young adult you wonder if you are supposed to acquire wisdom and when will your wisdom come forth. As the years go by, if you acquire wisdom, what do you do with it and where do you keep it? One of the reasons you keep wisdom is so you can pass it on to others . . . when asked.

Acknowledgments

Donna Reily Davis, Michelle Holt, Lindsay A. Hopper, Jeanelle McCall, Jack Paschtag, Read Hopkins Reily, Gina Renfro, Versia Sanders, Sheila Sutton, and photographer Becki Basham.

To three people who make everyone better by knowing them: Jim Smith who welcomed me every step of the way and for his constant patience; Vicki Ahl for her good cheer and flawless design; and Carl Condit for his enthusiasm.

Introduction

I was born at 3:13 pm in Dallas, Texas on August 7, 1934 which was recorded as one of the hottest summers in Texas history. My frail childhood encouraged my mother to provide a stairway for me to climb with a railing which I held onto for safety. Yet, with my natural athletic reflexes, I learned to ride my bicycle.

Raised with two brothers, at an early age I played neighborhood football with the boys. When my father saw all the boys take off their shirts during a backyard football game and saw me do the same, with a soft voice he advised, "Nancy, you don't take off your shirt too." I took piano lessons for eight years until my father asked, "Nancy, is this the best you can play." I replied, "Yes, Daddy." He said in a kind tone, "Why don't you quit." I did.

My high school career included intramural sports and the Highland Park Musical Festival Highland Fling dance routine on the football field. I failed to keep the musical beat and dropped out of the dance. I spent many summers on my aunt and uncle's ranch in New Mexico where the colorful landscape captured my heart.

My first paying job was addressing envelopes in a dress shop for fifty cents an hour. I graduated with honors from high school. While my friends went to the University of Texas, I was too naïve and attended Gulf Park College in Gulfport, Mississippi where I lettered in volleyball. One year of a girls' school was enough, so I transferred to Southern Methodist University where I was president of my sorority, an SMU yearbook beauty nominee and an intramural all-star field hockey goalie. I was now climbing the stairway holding onto the railings for security.

I met my husband on a blind date. When he told me good-night, I thought I'd never see him again because I was an hour late for the date, had a huge boil on the side of my nose, and he fell asleep in the movie. The next morning he called me for coffee and doughnuts.

My father died at age forty-six and I always miss his soft, guiding tone of voice. As a precursor for motherhood, I made a D in Child Development at SMU, but managed to graduate with honors with a B.B.A. in Retail Merchandising.

Upon my marriage to Donald E. Reily in 1955, with my husband a private in the United States Army, I held my second job as secretary to the quality control manager at Airpax Company in Baltimore, Maryland with my office next to the assembly line. When my husband was honorably discharged from the United States Army, we lived in Dallas for a short time and I gave birth to a son, Mark Hopkins Reily. I was now on my motherhood career walking on the stairway strong, sure and organizing the placement of the railings.

I then moved on a two-lane road from Dallas with a population of over 600,000 to my husband's home town, Corrigan, Texas with a population of less than one thousand, and one blinking traffic red light. A daughter, Donna Carolyn Reily, was born and my non-paying jobs included church parsonage chairman, PTA officer, United Fund raiser and home room mother.

To avoid more cultural shock we moved to Lufkin, Texas, with a population of approximately 23,000. Here I joined the Junior League, Museum of East Texas, and again the PTA. In the 1970s, after raising my two children, a yearning for creativity led to a career as an outdoor color portrait photographer which eventually led to writing.

My first book was without a computer and I literally "cut and pasted" sentences. With twenty years of research I published my second book, then a third, fourth and fifth one with a computer.

When my mother reached ninety-one years of age, I could not tell her good-bye, so I placed my hand on my dying mother's frail shoulder and told her, "Toodle-oo. I love you and there's more to be." When Don and I celebrated our fiftieth wedding anniversary he confessed that he stayed an extra year at SMU to work on his master's degree so he wouldn't lose me. From these experiences I maintained my presence for holding the stairway railing for safety, security, organization, and balance.

Along the way I gained wisdom.

—Nancy Hopkins Reily

For Women

For Women
While Waiting in Line for the Ladies' Rest Room

There is a fine art to being happy with what you have rather than being unhappy with what you don't have.

†

If you get mad you can get unmad in the same shoes.

†

One million dollars is not very much if you say "one million" fast.

†

She is so dumb she doesn't know "come here" from "sic 'em."

†

You talk my right arm off and whisper in the socket.

†

If you begin a sentence with "Please don't take this the wrong way," you probably don't need to say it.

†

Experience gives birth to opinion.

†

Your life is colored by your expectations.

†

Just because he or she is smart doesn't mean you are dumb.

†

Don't wear diamonds before noon unless you don't have them.

†

The worst serve as a bad example.

†

The first third of your life you want sex, the second third of your life you want status, the third part of your life you want security.

†

Why do all front fastening brassieres become back fastening?

†

Not everyone needs a padded brassiere.

†

Just when you think you have finished your work, a mother becomes a grandmother.

†

Be your husband's "mother" for only five minutes.

†

Behind every good man is a woman who is rolling her eyes.

†

With your grandchildren spending time with you during the summer you question whether you are running a "day camp" or a "bed and breakfast."

†

Don't let a perfectly good crisis go to waste.

†

Your guess is more accurate than a man's certainty.

†

The perfect dress length is at the smallest part of the leg—between the knee and the beginning of the calf.

†

Keep plucking your eyebrows and you will have none.

†

High heel shoes are not very sexy if you cry when they hurt your feet.

†

Surround yourself with people who love you.

†

Oh, for the days of equipment that was just "on" or "off."

†

You pay for your raising when you raise your own.

†

Research confirms: reduce calories to lose weight.

†

When my grandsons are too big to hug, I hug them anyway and say, "I'm gonna steal a hug."

†

Don't wear so much jewelry that everyone notices your jewelry rather than your smile.

†

The day is cold enough to wear two sleeves, but not three.

†

You are not in trouble until you get caught.

†

Motion pictures are the province of male fantasies.

†

Secrets when shared lose their power.

†

You need your glasses to just see your dreams at night.

†

My bosoms are not too small or too large, they are just my bosoms.

†

Low quality sleep saps your mental clarity.

†

There is a fine line of balance between a husband and wife that no one else knows about except those two.

†

Use tap water, not bottled water.

†

Everyone listens better to outside authorities.

†

Mute the television advertisements.

†

Nothing raises the odds of success more than experience.

†

Boosting your activity level increases your cognitive functions.

†

Is this a culture that tries to be happy even if it requires denial?

†

Five reasons to exercise: health, health, health, health, and health.

†

Paint used to be peach, blue, and brown. Now it's peach fuzz, peach slush, beach umbrella blue, midsummer's blue, pecan pie brown, and southern biscuit brown.

†

Three wise women ask for directions, get there on time, clean the stable, deliver the baby, prepare supper, give practical gifts to the baby and declare peace for all.

†

Louisiana doesn't drain very well.

†

That person doesn't know how to use an adding machine, much less plug it in.

†

Rest provides a good face lift.

†

Your wardrobe should be about practicality, not hope.

†

Don't ask your opera friends to go to a football game. You won't enjoy it and neither will they.

†

Don't pass gas downstairs.

†

The best skill you have as a homemaker is knowing how to load the dishwasher.

†

A lawsuit against you keeps you sharp.

†

Men are like streetcars, if you miss one, another one will be by shortly.

†

Leave the bathroom exhaust fan on for about fifteen minutes after the mirror fog disappears.

†

Try to do something challenging every day.

†

You choose to stew.

†

You didn't come to town with the first load of watermelons.

†

You will work for bread, but won't work for cake.

†

Eat right.

†

You may not always be happy, but you can be cheerful.

†

Your husband told you that if you ever want to run off, take him with you. Don't leave him with all the mess.

†

Nothing should last longer than it needs to.

†

You are deserving of a standing ovation for just getting through it.

†

You give back as much as you receive.

†

Mind your middle.

†

Your deeds don't go unnoticed.

†

Your silence doesn't go unnoticed.

†

Make friends.

†

Talking too much about doing something doesn't take the place of doing that something.

†

When you are young, be careful what furniture you take from others because you have it the remainder of your life.

†

Good advice a mother can give a daughter when she marries: "Don't put your hand on the lawnmower." Only years later did the true meaning come forth.

†

The eleventh commandment: "Don't take thyself so seriously."

†

It's enough to make a body tired.

†

A pesky husband is better than none at all.

†

In your marriage, care enough about each other to stay and fight it out.

†

In your marriage, does the good outweigh the bad?

†

Use your head for more than a hatband.

†

When you want to make more and more money it is a quest for power, then to want to make even more money is a cry for help.

†

Use it or lose it.

†

Horses sweat, men perspire, women dew.

After the "change of life" you get a "second wind."

†

She's so slow like molasses—slow following slow.

†

When you were middle aged, a young man told you, "The only thing looking old about you is that your purses are too big."

†

One thing we all have in common is trouble and television.

†

If you are consistently ten minutes late, you can be consistently ten minutes early, or consistently on time.

†

A man genuinely tries to please his woman, but you have to show him how.

†

You can accomplish a lot if you don't care who gets credit.

†

Having money is one thing, knowing what to do with money is something else.

†

There are more people without taste, than people with taste.

†

He is a man who can be trusted with your wife and wallet.

†

Be leery of any idea whose only merit is to avoid paying income taxes.

†

The best part of your life can't be put into words.

•

Work is the central theme of your life.

†

Free-be jobs are a dime a dozen.

†

You that tooteth not your own horn, the same shall remain tootless.

†

If you are in a bottomless hole put the shovel down and quit digging.

†

Get plenty of fresh air.

†

Get fifteen minutes of sunshine every day.

†

The day of the party, the hostess should take a nap.

†

Listen to others, then do what you feel is best.

†

If you always do what you always did, then you will always get what you always got.

†

Look outside the box and follow your dreams.

†

Anything you commit to do takes three times as long and costs twice as much.

†

Take the plastic off your new lamp shades.

†

Whatever you do, do it with all your might. Things done in halves are never done right.

†

Be patient.

†

Make an event a family event.

†

If you always tell the truth you don't have to remember what you said.

†

If one phase of your life is stressful, don't wish it away; the next phase may be more stressful.

†

Your possessions finally possess you.

†

Simplicity brings sereneness.

†

Gray hairs soften the lines of an old face.

†

The group is as fast as the slowest one.

†

If you become bored and drop the activity, then your life is cluttered with incomplete expressions.

†

Education without meaning or excitement is impossible.

†

An approach to teaching: if it's not right in every way, it's wrong.

†

Each morning when you awake, say "Self …"

†

Your life's direction goes according to your choices.

†

Wash down to nearly there and wash up to nearly there.

†

When a child falls asleep in your arms, it's an undeniably peaceful feeling.

†

To be kind is more important than to be right.

†

Never refuse a gift from a child.

†

In life's most serious moments, you need a friend to laugh with.

†

You need a person to hold your hand and a heart that listens.

†

The tiny daily events make your life so beautiful.

†

In times of stress, even the toughest want to be held.

†

If you know how to do something you will always have a job. If you know why something is done, you will be the boss.

†

A woman needs her own purse to move about, to move on, or to move out.

†

A woman needs youth she can leave behind.

†

Every woman should have a hammer, saw and a lacy black brassiere.

†

Your best friend lets you laugh or cry.

†

Your life wouldn't be so complicated if you didn't have so many lipsticks.

†

You need to know how to fall in love without losing yourself.

†

You should know how to work harder or just walk away.

†

People who talk a lot don't remember what all they say.

†

If you could have half of your wishes, you would double your trouble.

†

A mother's capacity for sacrifice is always amazing.

†

Fame must accompany honor, or fame is only like a small meteor whizzing through the sky throwing a transient light.

†

Fame with honor is like a bright light casting light everywhere.

†

You can vent your feelings with words, written or spoken.

†

On the Stage of Life, it's the conscience that claps and applauds.

†

Everything you see is subject to change.

†

You never sleep well before a trip because you are "journey proud."

†

You are over equipped with TV, DVD, digital cameras and iPhones for your ability.

†

She is a person who never disappoints those who expect the worst.

†

Whatever attracted you to your husband in the first place is usually what "drives you crazy" later.

†

If you don't think you are doing three things at one time, you think you are not being productive.

†

Keep your skin out of the harsh sun because you have more time to be old than young.

†

Lead, don't drive.

†

You like your bacon flat, crisp and organized.

†

If you live long enough you just about experience everything.

†

A gentlemen puts both commode lids down. A lady puts both commode lids down.

†

Be leery of people who groan all the time.

†

You inherit the body of your youth.

†

Life gets you where the hair is the shortest.

†

It's a great life, if you don't weaken.

†

When things are going smoothly, watch out because something is coming.

†

It's no sin to be poor but it's sure inconvenient.

†

Why does everyone dump on you? Because you are the mother.

†

Your daughter is too old for dolls, too young for gin.

†

You have a good sense of what the traffic will bear.

†

You can't put old heads on young shoulders.

†

One of life's greatest pleasures is to learn, equal to that is the pleasure you get when you "showoff" your grandchildren.

†

As the young rediscover the past, what is new, is really old.

†

There is always an elite within an elite.

†

To possess the ability to see further, as a visionary, and not let others have access to this thinking is to burn the spirit.

†

You need more than a "windshield survey."

†

Originality is forgetting where you acquired the idea.

†

You have two voices within you: one speaks from your heart, the other from your head. When they blend together you are closer to your vision of your dreams.

†

In all that you do and say, you must consider the end results.

†

Happiness derived from virtue is the best happiness.

†

You can't fault anyone for the aging process; everyone ages differently.

†

Your determination determines you even more.

†

Love is a choice.

†

It's just as easy to fall in love with a rich man as a poor man.

†

Your best talent is surrounding yourself with talented people.

†

If you follow someone else's path, you are neglecting your own path.

†

Revenge is not about getting back, but getting better.

†

It's no crime to say, "I don't know."

†

When you are walking somewhere, do you know how to amble?

†

Don't coast, there's not a moment to lose.

†

We need more statesmen than politicians.

†

When you are having a party, just before the party when you are doing a dozen things, you get "hostess heat."

†

Thoughts lead to words, words lead to actions, your actions can become habits. Your habits become character that leads to your destiny.

†

As parents of teenagers, you don't need to know everything they do.

†

Raise your children with good manners so each feels at ease having dinner at the White House or lunch on a picnic.

†

If you lose someone and keep talking about him/her, you don't lose them.

†

What is right for you, you will get. What is not right for you, you will not get.

†

Excellence is the best deterrent to gender, race, and age.

†

The more you complain, the more you find fault.

†

She wasn't ugly, only "hard favored."

†

When something is undone, something pushes you to fill in the blank spaces.

†

Don't live your life so that at the end, you feel like you have lived someone else's life.

†

The only trouble with golf is the nineteenth hole.

†

Eat slowly and keep both feet on the floor.

†

Do you want to be a pioneer woman and be among the first women to stop cooking?

†

What my children see at home is a barometer of what they can expect in their home.

†

A clean car drives better.

†

You always act better when you are dressed up.

†

Sometimes you feel like your dog chasing his tail and circling to find a good spot to lie down.

†

It's a talent to speak in perfect sentences, an art to speak in perfect paragraphs.

†

After you and your spouse achieve the American dream of a house and two cars in a two car garage, now comes the hard part: keeping your relationship together because you don't need each other as much.

†

Fake life until your joy returns.

†

An active mind doesn't sit still well.

†

If you ask to borrow something and you know that you don't return things, you are really asking someone to give you that item.

†

It takes a good mother to make a good daughter.

†

When you are lonesome you have no friends or family. When you are alone you have nothing to think about.

†

It's your choice to be late, early or on time.

†

If you think and speak of your friends or relatives as a house under construction, perhaps they will think and speak of you as the same.

†

It's an occupational hazard to worry about your children.

†

In your youth you were exclusive; in your aging you become inclusive because you don't want to be left out.

†

Every age has its crown of beauty.

†

When someone selling rocks meets someone buying rocks is when two fools meet.

†

In old age when you can't think of something, it is when your brain farts.

†

Do you live so far from town that the sun rises between your house and town?

†

A flat roof never leaks when it's not raining.

†

Always buy your young grandchildren the same color of play balls so they won't fight over who gets what color.

†

What's not in a journal is as important as what's in a journal.

†

There is trouble and then there is trouble.

†

Wearing thong underwear is like having a wedgie all day long.

†

Perfect practice makes perfect.

†

Being a lady never goes out of style.

†

You don't appreciate someone else's work, until you do it yourself.

†

For some it's easier to see what is not clean, than what is clean.

†

When you are mad you have to chose how far you want to force someone into a corner. The more you do, the further in the corner you are. You have to come out eventually, or else.

†

Life is just simpler if you go by the rules.

†

It is easier to give instructions than to follow instructions.

†

You watch your parents master the good and bad times in their marriage and try to emulate them.

†

You don't want to live so long that when you die, all they say is, "It's a blessing."

†

You try not to swap holes with your money.

†

When you are driving on a dusty road and encounter a person walking, slow down so they won't eat your dust.

†

When you go through a ranch gate, leave the gate as you found it.

†

The first baby takes only seven months, the others nine months.

†

Marriage is not what you thought it would be.

†

Hell hath no fury like a woman. He knows this, so why does he do the things he does.

†

Your role as mother to a grown child is simply to listen.

†

You don't like to spend the night any place that isn't as nice as your house.

†

You are yourself an original not a copy.

†

You can do a lot more than you think you can.

†

Try to avoid negative people.

†

An epic journey is a once in a lifetime experience.

†

Enjoy the detours.

†

Complaining is for the small-minded people.

†

Perseverance saves the day.

†

Did you list your goals far short of your potential?

†

What people think of you is not as important as what you know of yourself.

†

Smile.

†

Your athletic challenges come in second to the insights you gain.

†

There is no such day as a bad-weather day, only your inappropriate clothing for the day.

†

You receive gladly what others offer you. It may be their best they can offer.

†

The desire to prepare trains you for the desire to prevail.

†

Your friends are so important to you, you wish they all knew each other.

†

After a mishap, get moving.

†

In your youth start mixing the colors and brush strokes to be a fine, lovable old person.

†

The good finds good; the bad finds bad.

†

You are what you eat.

†

Your ancestors gave you your eye and hair color; your attitude and sweat makes you what you are.

†

Do your best for the moment.

†

The state of your heart determines how happy you are.

†

Quality is the best bargain.

†

Knowledge is power.

†

To wish away one phase of life may result in a worse next one.

†

You are responsible for your part of the world.

†

Your bad habits broken make your part of the world better.

†

Play life to win.

†

The law of averages will surface sooner or later.

†

If you regret your mistakes you still have a chance.

†

If you can soothe an emotional ache by listening to someone else, you'll be needed.

†

Adversity calls for humility.

†

If you always do what's right, you need not worry your conscience.

†

Much is gained by practice, not preaching.

†

Right is the solution, wrong is the problem.

†

Love softens any heart.

†

You rule yourself for the good rewards.

†

Each age comes in the right sequence.

†

An objective not too high or too low ends in a fine achievement.

†

Manners keep you civilized and have no language barrier.

†

Loyalty substitutes for many weaknesses.

†

Honesty is a right due its own reward.

†

Only mankind blushes.

†

Born outer beauty fades into an exquisite inward beauty.

†

You must ponder to hear the voice in the silence.

†

Self-reliance can make a go of inspiration, courage and effort.

†

Work is the central theme of your life.

†

Today is your best day.

†

The pessimist missed the sunset for the long shadows.

†

You did your best.

†

Risks keep life interesting.

†

Your attitude toward money makes it servant or master.

†

It's not what you say, but your tone of voice.

†

Barking friends you don't need.

†

You give yourself a financial raise by lowering your expenses.

†

Not everyone knows how to handle money.

†

What you see is different from what others see.

†

Be yourself—your only role in life.

†

Your aptitudes used make you happier.

†

Your health is your first priority.

†

Love alternates between slowly doubting, irritating, accusing, criticizing and quickly believing, approval, laughter and excusing.

†

To sleep well lightens your burdens.

†

Bad friends bring bad days.

†

Faithfulness resides in small and great matters.

†

To have is to exert effort.

†

Did you quit too soon?

†

Common sense can outrun money.

†

Loyalty keeps us in the right direction.

†

You treasure the rights of others.

†

Read something each day.

†

We all have teaching tongues.

†

You run the risk of poor judgment each time you make a choice, but your motive keeps judgment in perspective.

†

Progress is made in three steps forward, one backward step, two forward steps, and this makes you a winner for trying.

†

Stickability.

†

A wrong to you has no home unless you choose to remember.

†

You hope to wise up before your school is dismissed.

†

Living a day by chance increases the odds for failure.

†

You are stalled when you can't decide yes or no and may lose tomorrow.

†

Goals add the zest to life.

†

You are prettier for struggles rising above prickly ugliness.

†

The thought of an easy life left you unprepared for reality.

†

To expect defeat puts you almost there.

†

Guilt is your braking system.

†

Feelings are not facts.

†

One boy is one boy; two boys is half a boy; three boys is no boys.

†

Am I getting myself?

†

Skinny is good, but missing a lot.

†

Do you want to die on this hill?

†

There are skirmishes, battles and wars. You can lose all the skirmishes; lose half the battles; but you need to win all the wars.

†

You can't see the stars when your head is down.

†

You need sorrow in small increments, joy in larger increments.

†

You are marked by what you say and what you don't say.

†

To understand where others come from is an art in itself.

†

You work harder at controlling your dog than yourself.

†

Life is easier if you follow the rules.

†

A clear conscience is no prison.

†

A slanderer has no friends except his king.

†

You give your friend the quiet confidence in you that he needs.

†

Your gray hair and gray matter give you double power; add enthusiasm and you triple your power.

†

Your smile in the early morning mirror you see only once, others should see it all day.

†

The world looks better through your better eyes.

†

Are you sweet because sugar was mixed with your dust?

†

The more you see and hear evil, the less evil it seems.

†

As a glory seeker you are a sorry attraction.

†

You cherish self-esteem over public opinion.

†

Begin.

†

Success requires action.

†

You seek a mature person.

†

To laugh at yourself qualifies you as an adult.

†

It's a stretch when you read material "over your head."

†

You know you are an adult when you need naps.

†

You find peace in pursuing a passion.

†

Tears are understood in any language.

†

Giving birth to your child gives you a lifelong purpose.

†

Wake up to the fast-breaking day, free to receive it with the tick of your heart.

†

You are wise if your know your vulnerabilities.

†

Time changes the calendar of circumstances.

†

You gather around cheerful people.

†

To listen is to be a friend.

†

The price of wisdom is getting older.

†

A thorn in your side can be an actual blessing.

†

Another person's appearance may deceive and not be worthy of envy.

†

Fault finding in another may be a way to lose.

†

A tombstone praises the one below.

†

Today is yours.

†

Concentrate, stay focused.

†

Home is a safe harbor.

†

No Fridays for a mother.

†

The squeak in your back door told you of your children's comings and goings.

†

Love is a choice you make daily.

†

If you had a dog, you'd never ask for trouble by picking him up by the ears.

†

How much do you listen to those who say you're too young or too old to do something?

†

A simple solution: right vs. wrong.

†

You've never seen a monument to a fault-finder.

†

Your disappointments teach you a better way.

†

Hocus-pocus won't solve your problems.

†

Variety.

†

There must be a way.

†

You let your friend breathe.

†

Short legs, if used wisely, can win over long legs used unwisely.

†

A lengthy report can probably be written on a 4 x 6 inch note card.

†

A mother teaches the best principles.

†

Being a mother brings forth emotions you don't know you owned, much less expressed.

†

The child who received a good upbringing becomes the same parent.

†

Truth outweighs all rumors.

†

The golden thread of life is a little shorter each day.

†

A sleepless night always ends.

†

It's better for your descendants to have something to brag about than for you to brag about your ancestors.

†

A soft heart makes a soft nighttime pillow.

†

You must learn the causes.

†

You are a good dishwasher if you dry them clean.

†

If employed, abstinence of anything gets easier.

†

If you don't reach all of today's goals, you're still ahead if you don't set any goals.

✝

Your reputation is not the same as your character.

✝

Trust.

✝

Too many character flaws won't support a strong life.

✝

Handle with care.

✝

Truth is immortal.

✝

No idea is bad because it's old, no idea is good because it's new.

✝

Think.

✝

He still says, "What's for supper?"

✝

Silence can be the loudest voice.

✝

Be practical to avoid stumped toes.

✝

You are young if your heart has no wrinkles.

✝

Business before pleasure.

✝

Swearing is a habit.

✝

Pride precedes a fall.

✝

The snooze button serves no purpose but to delay.

✝

Do you need a rumor cemetery?

✝

As a teacher you know more than others and others know more than you.

✝

Manners pay off.

†

He is a man by life.

†

She is a woman by life.

†

You measure your age by attitude, not years.

†

Be self-loyal.

†

Be yourself, not the tail on another dog.

†

You can end an argument by saying, "Last word."

†

Thank you.

†

If you follow someone, you must know his/her path.

†

Do your best.

†

Anticipate.

†

Do your homework, even after the wedding ceremony.

†

You conquer your faults one fault at a time.

†

You like books that make you think.

†

A big person rules his many smalls.

†

Bankers are leery of a pick-up truck and horse trailer in matching colors.

†

A clock ticks louder on a sleepless night.

†

You never ask your maid to do anything you won't do.

†

Think to be a leader.

†

Praise invigorates.

†

You don't tell jokes if you can't tell them effortlessly.

†

All offend: a fart, a fart inadequately disguised by a burnt match, and a fart joke.

†

To face your estranged friend or relative shrinks your differences.

†

You seldom aggravate strife or it grows bigger.

†

You've never seen a human with a halo.

†

To be merciful is to sparkle like a rainbow.

†

To get you must give.

†

The stars sparkle in silence, so can you.

†

Your habits take you down a path.

†

Quality is the best bargain.

†

The rich man practices thrift. That's why he's rich.

†

To honk your horn at a person draws attention to you.

†

Your children marry who they know.

†

Speed bumps are for all.

†

You will always need a link to others.

†

Revenge is self-wounding.

†

Harping is a discordant tune.

†

Play life to the conclusion.

†

Why aren't homemakers paid for their work? Because no one could afford them.

†

The devil is in the details.

†

When driving a car, what is the condition where you can stop on a railroad track? None.

†

Character is what you are when you are in the dark, when nobody is watching.

†

When you are angry you become the victim, poor you, and you are at your weakest.

†

When you are mad or pout, after a while no one really cares.

†

You don't care if you look fat or thin or rich or poor, but thin and rich is better.

†

You never ask for your parent's advice until you get in trouble.

†

If you think things couldn't get worse, you either drown or pull yourself above the waterline, which brings peace.

†

You train to be a participant, not an observer.

†

Your child doesn't want to know about his/her mother, but wants to know her.

†

You want to be the role model for your daughter she needs, not the role model you think you should be.

†

There is an art to placing your children in the right place at the right time.

†

When you give someone a gift, the first recipient is you.

†

Mistakes are a gift.

†

You adjourn the board of directors' meeting, then you decide what to do.

†

If your only tool is a hammer, then all your problems are the nails.

†

You know your child was growing up when he learned to say "no."

†

You seat your least favorite dinner guest at the table below the salt.

†

It's not what you know, but who you know.

†

The success of your marriage is that you never discuss anything serious.

†

The three things you don't discuss in polite society: politics, religion and sex. But you vote, go to church, and have children.

†

You can't undo the sound of a bell after you ring it.

†

There is a very thin line between being opinionated, cynical, and mean.

†

Whoever angers you, controls you.

†

Rules without consequences are merely suggestions.

✝

Consequences applied inconsistently are called random acts of nature. It's hard to learn from consequences if you apply them inconsistently and randomly.

✝

The only way you can have peace is to take it.

✝

Life is all about your choices.

✝

Desire is a marvelous feeling followed by love.

✝

You can walk without going to others.

✝

After you have been married a while, you discover you are not married to you, but to a completely different person than yourself.

✝

You understand things only in relief.

✝

The beauty of your life is in today.

✝

If you have a vision, you can plan and go forward.

✝

Bought sense is better than borrowed sense.

✝

The quest of revenge is control.

✝

You pay for love with grief.

✝

For a case of shingles, cover each bud with clear nail polish.

✝

For night leg cramps, put a bar of soap (not Dove or Dial) under your bottom bed sheet. Replace the soap in six weeks.

✝

The complainer would rather vent than listen.

✝

Life gets harder, the farther you go.

✝

You can be stronger than you think you can be.

†

What you say "goes" and you say "go."

†

You try to be good except when it's to your advantage not to be good.

†

When you are right, that is all you get to be.

†

You must seize the opportunity of a lifetime during the lifetime of the opportunity.

†

It's not how you fall, but how you get up.

†

A banker says, "You can't die now, you owe the bank."

†

When buying new shoes, try on the left foot in the early afternoon when you feet aren't swollen.

†

After others have let go, hold on.

†

Your victory over life is how many lives you have touched.

†

Your net worth is living it and driving it.

†

You work hard rather than hardly working.

†

You reserve the right to be "wishy-washy."

†

You became creative when you couldn't do anything else.

†

Applaud only when the symphony conductor turns to face the audience and don't stand up.

†

He works hard but not smart-hard.

†

You try to not be "knee-walking drunk."

†

You used all your drink tickets.

†

You know just how much to pour and still be dignified.

†

The language of love is dance and plenty of it.

†

You are happiest when your "To Do List" is short.

†

College is a learning curve for the parents and student.

†

If someone doesn't know how old you are, how old does that person think you are?

†

A man courts a woman until she's won and a woman wants to be won every day.

†

Death gives value to every day.

†

A woman doesn't give her children in marriage, but shares them with their spouse.

†

A little help to someone can make all the difference.

†

Your passion should cool before action.

†

Verbal self-defense is a law of nature.

†

Ambition that is ungovernable should be noted.

†

History is a group of ironies.

†

Remember to pull the little stickers off the bananas, lemons, and apples.

†

You don't fool your dentist if you don't floss.

†

Family is who you call when you are in trouble.

†

Men are as complex as women.

†

Outlaw power tools for your spouse.

†

Your work is the most rewarding if you already have money.

†

College taught you how to get along with people.

†

Silence is so accurate.

†

Most of what you do is mundane. You live for the ten percent of life that is memorable.

†

You are old enough to call your mother on your birthday and wish her a happy day.

†

To cut your credit card debt: quit charging, write down what you owe, ask for a lower interest rate, switch cards, exceed the minimum payment, save, and make additional income.

†

As you get older, you move less and observe more.

†

When you die has your presence been enough to move some to tears?

†

You are pleased when your children are known as your children, not so when you're known as their mother.

†

If you are naked and smiling, you guess he's a lucky man.

†

Your body is like your face: it tells a story of who you are and how you feel about it.

†

Can't beat being naked and laughing.

†

The lessons to learn just keep coming.

†

An assessment comes with experience.

†

It's not just about taking care of the planet, it's also about taking care of yourself.

†

The real beginning of happiness is gratitude.

†

Keep on truckin', sit quietly and listen, judgment is judgment, and "letting go" begins at your birth.

†

The most powerful person at the dinner table sits on your right.

†

Don't spend time stalking a turtle.

†

Your soul knows no age.

†

Does your bathing suit bring out the best in body satisfaction?

†

You need a brassiere if when standing naked you can place a pencil horizontally beneath one breast and the pencil doesn't fall.

†

Life is life anywhere.

†

De-stress by breathing: inhale to a count of four, hold that breath for a count of seven and then exhale to a count of eight.

†

Take the stairs.

†

As your face wrinkles, go the European way and age with dignity rather than the Hollywood plasticity.

†

There should be equal parts of giving and taking.

†

The United States flag should be displayed on the left from the viewing public.

†

Heroes are made in an instant.

†

Do abstract or theory ideas interfere with thinking to confuse an issue?

†

Every consequence has a cause, so find out the cause to change the effect.

†

It's the crisis that distinguishes you and allows you to surpass others.

†

Be bigger than the temptation that is attempting to destroy you.

†

Home is where the mother is.

†

Why do men and only men back into parking spots?

†

The journey up from adversity can be exhilarating and exhausting.

†

When is their artfulness in clothes?

†

You don't see the etiquette rules until they are broken.

†

Wear a bikini in August and look forward to buying and wearing a winter coat.

†

You need to differentiate between stylish versus fashionable.

†

Just because it's "ready to wear" doesn't mean it's not beautiful.

†

In your physical presence and clothes avoid a "statement-y" look.

†

There is a difference between bad behavior and bad taste.

†

You want to quit when the room is full of people.

†

You grew to your wisdom.

†

Just finish.

†

You have all this wisdom, but no one wants it.

†

Give wisdom a chance.

For Men

For Men

At the Men's Latrine

Whatever you anticipate, just begin.

†

Success requires action.

†

A grown-ass man doesn't show his underwear in public.

†

Don't pass gas downstairs.

†

If you begin a sentence with "Please don't take this the wrong way," you probably don't need to say it.

†

Talking about something too long does not take the place of doing that something.

†

There is a fine art to being happy with what you have, rather than being unhappy with what you don't have.

†

Rest.

†

You are equal to others when you sleep.

†

When you want to make more, more and more money it is a quest for power, then to want to make even more money is a cry for help.

†

Why do men take traffic stop signs, red lights and speed bumps as mere suggestions?

†

How about chocolate for a tooth cavity filling?

†

You don't want your spouse, at the end of her life, to realize she had lived someone else's life.

†

Why do men and only men back into parking spots.

†

Don't let a perfectly good crisis go to waste.

†

Oh, for the days of equipment with just "on or off."

†

Anyone can borrow money, but not everyone can pay it back.

†

If you compliment a woman friend in front of your wife, be sure you have complimented your wife earlier.

†

Just when you think you can retire, a father becomes a grandfather.

†

Don't make passes at girls that have on glasses, unless that's all they have on.

†

One million dollars is not very much if you say "one million" fast.

†

There is a fine line of balance between a husband and wife that no one knows about except the husband and wife.

†

Everyone listens better to outside authorities.

†

Experience gives birth to opinion.

†

Louisiana doesn't drain very well.

†

Any man's tie is pretty if it has red in it.

†

Why does an automobile speedometer go higher than legal speed limits or faster than the car will go? It's a marketing and sales gimmick to make the driver think he could go faster and is exerting restraint.

†

Death ends your life, but not your relationship.

†

Motion pictures are the province of male fantasies.

†

You are not in trouble until you get caught.

†

Low quality sleep saps your mental clarity.

†

To save gasoline, don't idle your car.

†

Use tap water.

†

There is less vibration in a ceiling fan that has five blades rather than four.

†

Mute the television advertisements.

†

Secrets when shared lose their power.

†

Nothing raises the odds of success more than experience.

†

You need your glasses to just see your dreams at night.

†

Boosting your activity level increases your cognitive functions.

†

You don't want to dress so that others notice your clothes rather than the smile on your face.

†

That person doesn't know how to use an adding machine, much less plug it in.

†

Your life is colored by expectations.

†

She is so dumb she doesn't know "come here" from "sic 'em."

†

Your wardrobe should be about practicality, not hope.

†

Leave the bathroom exhaust fan on for about fifteen minutes after the mirror fog disappears.

†

Research confirms that you need to reduce calories to lose weight.

†

Five reasons to exercise: health, health, health, health, and health.

†

Paint used to be named peach, blue, and brown. Now it's peach fuzz, peach slush, beach umbrella blue, midsummer's blue, pecan pie brown, and southern biscuit brown.

†

Are you in a culture that tries to be happy even if it requires denial?

†

She talks your right arm off and whispers in the socket.

†

Just because the other person is smart doesn't mean you are dumb.

†

The success of your marriage is that you both never discuss anything serious.

†

The three things not to discuss in public: politics, sex and religion. Yet, you voted, had children and went to church.

†

Marriage is not what you thought it would be.

†

The worst serve as a bad example.

†

You pay for your raising when you raise your own.

†

If you get mad, you can get unmad in the same shoes.

†

Eat right.

†

Mind your middle.

†

You don't ask your opera friends to go to a football game. You won't enjoy it and neither will they.

†

When you snow ski, don't yell at skiers going down hill.

†

Try to do something challenging every day.

†

Your children marry who they know.

†

A lawsuit against you keeps you sharp.

†

Loyalty is a pocketbook thick.

†

You choose to stew.

†

Use it or lose it.

†

You didn't come to town with the first load of watermelons.

†

You will work for bread, but you won't work for cake.

†

You may not always be happy, but you can be cheerful.

†

If you ever want to run off, take your wife with you. Don't leave her with all the mess.

†

Nothing should last longer than it needs to.

†

You were deserving of a standing ovation for just getting through it.

†

You give back as much as you receive.

†

Make friends.

†

Your deeds don't go unnoticed.

†

Your silence doesn't go unnoticed.

†

Talking too much about doing something doesn't take the place of doing that something.

†

When you are young, be careful what hand-me-down furniture you take from others because you will have it the remainder of your life.

†

Get fresh air.

†

It's enough to make a body tired.

†

A pesky wife is better than none at all.

†

In your marriage, care enough about each other to stay and fight it out.

†

In your marriage, the good outweighs the bad.

†

As you age you need to not let your idiosyncrasies take control.

†

Are you using your head for more than a hatband?

†

Horses sweat, men perspire, women dew.

†

She's so slow like molasses, slow following slow.

†

One thing we all have in common is trouble and television.

†

If you are consistently ten minutes late, you can be consistently ten minutes early or consistently on time.

†

A man genuinely tries to please a woman, but a woman has to show him how.

†

You can accomplish a lot if you don't care who gets the credit.

†

Make any event a family event.

†

Having money is one thing, knowing what to do with money is something else.

†

There are more people without taste, than people with taste.

†

He is a man who can be trusted with your wife and wallet.

†

Be leery of any idea whose only merit is to avoid paying income taxes.

†

The best part of your life can't be put into words.

†

Work is the central theme of your life.

†

Free-be jobs are a dime a dozen.

†

You that tooteth not your own horn, the same shall remain tootless.

†

If you are in a bottomless hole, put down the shovel or get off the backhoe and quit digging.

†

Listen to others, then do what you feel is best.

†

If you always do what you always did, then you will always get what you always got.

†

Look outside the box and follow your dreams.

†

Anything you ever commit to do takes three times as long and costs twice as much.

†

Whatever you do, do it with all your might. Things done in halves are never done right.

†

Be patient.

†

If you always tell the truth you don't have to remember what you said.

†

If one phase of your life is stressful, don't wish it away; the next phase may be more stressful.

†

Your possessions finally possess you.

†

Simplicity brings sereneness.

†

The group is as fast as the slowest one.

†

If you become bored and drop the activity, then your life is cluttered with incomplete expressions.

†

Education without meaning or excitement is impossible.

†

An approach to teaching: if it's not right in every way, it's wrong.

†

Each morning when you awake, say, "Self ..."

†

Your life's direction goes according to your choices.

†

You wash down to nearly there and wash up to nearly there.

†

When a child falls asleep in your arms, it's an undeniable peaceful feeling.

†

To be kind is more important than to be right.

†

Never refuse a gift from a child.

†

In life's most serious moments, you need a friend to laugh with.

†

You only need a person to hold your hand and a heart that listens.

†

The tiny daily events make your life beautiful.

†

In times of emotional stress, even the toughest want to be held.

†

If you know how to do something you will always have a job. If you know why something is done you will be the boss.

†

A woman needs her own purse to move about, to move on or move out.

†

A man needs youth he can leave behind.

†

Your best friend lets you laugh or cry.

†

You need to know how to fall in love without losing yourself.

†

You should know how to work harder or just walk away.

†

People who talk a lot don't remember what all they say.

†

If you could have half of your wishes, you would double your trouble.

†

A father's capacity for sacrifice is always amazing.

†

Fame must accompany honor or fame is like a small meteor whizzing through the sky throwing only traveling, transient light.

†

Fame with honor is like a bright light casting light everywhere.

†

You can vent your feelings with written or spoken words.

†

On the Stage of Life, it's the conscience that claps and applauds.

†

Everything that you see is liable to change.

†

You never sleep well before a trip because you are "journey proud."

†

You are over equipped with TV, DVD, digital cameras and iPhones for your ability.

†

He is a person who never disappoints those who expect the worst.

†

Whatever attracted you to your wife in the first place is usually what "drives you crazy" later.

†

If you don't think you are doing three things at one time, you think you are not being productive.

†

Lead, don't drive.

†

A scrapbook can take on a life beyond its original concept.

†

You like your bacon flat, crisp and organized.

†

If you live long enough you just about experience everything.

†

A gentlemen puts both commode lids down when finished. A lady puts both commode lids down when finished.

†

Be leery of people who groan all the time.

†

Life gets you where the hair is the shortest.

†

It's a great life, if you don't weaken.

†

When things are going smoothly, watch out because something is coming.

†

It's no sin to be poor, but it's sure inconvenient.

†

Why does everyone dump on you? Because you are the father.

†

Your daughter is too old for dolls, too young for gin.

†

You have a good sense of what the traffic will bear.

†

You can't put old heads on young shoulders.

†

Always let your son win on one issue.

†

One of life's greatest pleasures is to learn. Equal to that pleasure is to "show off" your grandchildren.

†

As the young rediscover the past, what is new, is really old.

†

There is always an elite within an elite.

†

To possess the ability to see further, as a visionary, and not let others have access to this thinking is to burn the spirit.

†

You need more than a "windshield survey."

†

Originality is forgetting where you got the idea.

†

You have two voices within you. One speaks from your heart, the other from your head. When they blend together you are closer to your vision of your dreams.

†

In all that you do and say, you must consider the end results.

†

Happiness derived from virtue is the best happiness.

†

You can't fault anyone for their aging process. Everyone ages differently.

†

Your determination determines you even more.

†

Love is a choice.

†

It's just as easy to fall in love with a rich woman as a poor woman.

†

Your best talent is surrounding yourself with talented people.

†

If you follow someone else's path, you are neglecting your own path.

†

Revenge is not about getting back, but getting better.

†

It's no crime to say, "I don't know."

†

When you are walking somewhere, do you know how to amble?

†

Don't coast, there's not a moment to lose.

†

We need more statesmen than politicians.

†

Aging is a lot of output, but little gain.

†

Thoughts lead to words, words lead to actions, your actions can become habits. Your habits become character that lead to your destiny.

†

As parents of teenagers, you don't need to know everything they do.

†

You raise your children so each will feel at ease having dinner at the White House or having lunch on a picnic.

†

Your possessions finally possess you.

†

If you lose someone and keep talking about her, you don't lose her.

†

What is right for you, you will get. What is not right for you, you will not get.

†

Excellence is the best deterrent to gender, race, and age.

†

The more you complain, the more you find fault.

†

She wasn't ugly, only "hard favored."

†

When something is undone, something pushes you to fill in the blank spaces.

†

Don't live your life so that at the end you feel like you have lived someone else's life.

†

The only trouble with golf is the nineteenth hole.

†

Eat slowly and keep both feet on the floor.

†

What your children see at home is a barometer of what they can expect in their home.

†

A clean car drives better.

†

You always act better when you are dressed up.

†

Sometimes you feel like your dog chasing his tail, circling to find a good spot to lie down.

†

It's a talent to speak in perfect sentences, an art to speak in perfect paragraphs.

†

After you and your wife achieve the American dream of a house and two cars in a two car garage, now comes the hard part: keeping your relationship together because you don't need each other as much.

†

Fake life until your joy returns.

†

An active mind doesn't sit still well.

†

If you ask to borrow something from someone and you know that you don't return things, you are really asking that person to give you that item.

†

It takes a good father to make a good son.

†

When you are lonesome you have no friends or family. When you are alone you have nothing to think about.

†

It's your choice to be late, early or on time.

†

If you think and speak of your friends or relatives as a house under construction, perhaps they will think and speak of you as the same.

†

It's an occupational hazard to worry about your children.

†

In your youth you were exclusive; in your aging you become inclusive because you didn't want to be left out.

†

Every age has its crown of beauty.

†

When someone selling rocks meets someone buying rocks is when two fools meet.

†

You live so far from town that the sun rises between your house and town.

†

A flat roof never leaks when it's not raining.

†

You always buy your young grandchildren the same color of play balls, so they won't fight over who gets which color of ball.

†

There is trouble and then there is trouble.

†

Perfect practice makes perfect.

†

Being a gentleman never goes out of style.

†

You don't appreciate someone else's work, until you do it yourself.

†

For some it's easier to see what is not clean, than what is clean.

†

When you are mad you have to chose how far you want to force someone in the corner. The more you do the further in the corner you are. You have to come out eventually, or else.

†

Life is just simpler if you go by the rules.

†

It is easier to give instructions than to follow instructions.

†

You watch your parents master the good and bad times in their marriage and try to emulate them.

†

You don't want to live so long that when you die, all they say is "It's a blessing."

†

You try not to swap holes with your money.

†

When you are driving on a dusty road and encounter a person walking, slow down so they won't eat your dust.

†

When you go through a ranch gate, leave the gate as you found it.

†

The first baby takes only seven months, the others nine months.

†

Hell hath no fury like a woman, you know this, so why do you do the things you do.

†

Your parents said you never come to them for advice until you get into trouble.

†

Your role as father to a grown child is simply to listen.

†

You don't like to spend the night anyplace that isn't as nice as your house.

†

You are yourself an original, not a copy.

†

You can do a lot more than you think you can.

†

Try to avoid negative people.

†

An epic journey is a once in a lifetime experience.

†

Enjoy the detours.

†

Complaining is for small-minded people.

†

Perseverance saves the day.

†

You list your goals short of your potential.

†

What people think of you is not as important as what you know of yourself.

†

Smile.

†

Your athletic challenges come in second to the insights you gain.

†

There is no such day as a bad-weather day, only your inappropriate clothing for the day.

†

You receive gladly what others offer you. It may be the best they can offer.

†

The desire to prepare trains you for the desire to prevail.

†

Your friends are so important to you, you wish they all knew each other.

†

After a mishap, get moving.

†

In your youth, start mixing the colors and brush strokes to be a fine, lovable old person.

†

The good finds good; the bad finds bad.

†

You are what you eat.

†

Your ancestors gave you your eye and hair color; your attitude and sweat make you what you are.

†

Do your best for the moment.

†

The state of your heart determines how wise and happy you are.

†

When you chose a wife, your head and heart must agree.

†

Quality is the best bargain.

†

It takes two to argue.

†

To wish away one phase of life may result in a worse next one.

†

You are responsible for your part of the world.

†

Your bad habits broken make your part of the world better.

†

Play life to win.

†

The law of averages will surface sooner or later.

†

If you regret your mistakes you still have a chance.

†

If you can soothe an ache by listening, you'll be needed.

†

Adversity calls for humility.

†

If you always do what's right, you need not worry your conscience.

†

Much is to be gained by practice, not preaching.

†

Right is the solution, wrong is the problem.

†

Love softens any heart.

†

You rule yourself for the good rewards.

†

Each age comes in the right sequence.

†

An objective not too high or too low ends in a fine achievement.

†

Manners keep you civilized and have no language barriers.

†

Loyalty substitutes for many weaknesses.

†

Honesty is a right due its own reward.

†

Only mankind blushes.

†

You must ponder to hear the voice in the silence.

†

Self-reliance can make good inspiration, courage and effort.

†

Work is the central theme of your life.

†

Today is your best day.

†

The pessimist missed the sunset for the long shadows.

†

You did your best.

†

Risks keep life interesting.

†

Your attitude toward money makes it servant or master.

†

It's not what you say, but your tone of voice.

†

Barking friends you don't need.

†

You give yourself a financial raise by lowering your expenses.

†

Not everyone knows how to handle money.

†

What you see is different from what others see.

†

Be yourself—your only role in life.

†

Your aptitudes used make you happier.

†

Your health is your first priority.

†

Love alternates between slowly doubting, irritating, accusing, criticizing and quickly believing, approval, laughter and excusing.

†

To sleep well lightens your burdens.

†

Bad friends bring bad days.

†

Faithfulness resides in small and great matters.

†

To have is to exert effort.

†

Did you quit too soon?

†

Common sense can out run money.

†

Loyalty keeps you in the right direction.

†

You treasure the rights of others.

†

Read something each day.

†

Everyone has teaching tongues.

†

You run the risk of poor judgment each time you make a choice, but your motive keeps judgment in perspective.

†

Progress is made in three steps forward, one step backward, and two forward steps and this makes you a winner for trying.

†

Stickability.

†

A wrong to you has no home unless you choose to remember.

†

You hope to wise up before your school is dismissed.

†

Living a day by chance increases the odds for failure.

†

You stall when you can't decide "yes" or "no" and may lose tomorrow.

†

Goals add the zest to life.

†

You are more handsome for the struggles rising above prickly ugliness.

†

The thought of an easy life left you unprepared for reality.

†

To expect defeat puts you almost there.

†

Guilt is your braking system.

†

Guilt is a learned emotion because you are not born feeling guilty.

†

Feelings are not facts.

†

One boy is one boy; two boys is half a boy; three boys is no boys.

†

Are you getting yourself?

†

Skinny is good, but missing a lot.

†

Do you want to die on this hill?

†

There are skirmishes, battles and wars. You can lose all the skirmishes; lose half the battles; but, you need to win all the wars.

†

You can't see the stars when your head is down.

†

You need sorrow in small increments, joy in larger increments.

†

You are marked by what you say and what you don't say.

†

To understand where others come from is an art in itself.

†

You work harder at controlling your dog than yourself.

†

Life is easier if you follow the rules.

†

A clear conscience is no prison.

†

A slanderer has no friends except his king.

†

You give your friend the quiet confidence in you that he needs.

†

Your smile in the early morning mirror you see only once, others should see it all day.

†

The world looks better through your better eyes.

†

Are you sweet because sugar was mixed with your dust?

†

The more you see and hear evil, the less evil it seems.

†

As a glory seeker you are a sorry attraction.

†

You cherish self-esteem over public opinion.

†

You seek a mature person.

†

To laugh at yourself qualifies you as an adult.

†

It's a stretch when you read material "over your head."

†

You find peace in pursuing a passion.

†

Tears are understood in any language.

†

Having a child gives you a lifelong purpose.

†

Wake up to the fast-breaking day, free to receive it with the tick of your heart.

†

Knowledge is power.

†

You are wise if you know your vulnerabilities.

†

Time changes the calendar of circumstances.

†

You gather around cheerful people.

†

To listen is to be friends.

†

The price of wisdom is getting older.

†

A thorn in your side can be an actual blessing.

†

Another person's appearance may deceive and not be worthy of envy.

†

Fault finding in another may be a way to lose.

†

A tombstone praises the one below.

†

Today is yours.

†

Concentrate, stay focused.

†

Home is a safe harbor.

†

Love is a choice you make daily.

†

If you had a dog, you'd never ask for trouble by picking him up by the ears.

†

How much do you listen to those who say you're too young or too old to do something?

†

A simple solution is right versus wrong.

†

You've never seen a monument to a fault-finder.

†

Your disappointments teach you a better way.

†

Hocus-pocus won't solve your problems.

†

Variety.

†

There must be a way.

†

You let your friend breathe.

†

Short legs, if used wisely, can win over long legs used unwisely.

†

A lengthy report can probably be written on a 4 x 6 inch note card.

†

When you tell the truth you don't have to remember what you said.

†

A father teaches the best principles.

†

Being a father brings forth emotions you didn't know you owned, much less expressed.

†

The child who received a good upbringing becomes the same parent.

†

Truth outweighs all rumors.

†

The golden thread of life is a little shorter each day.

†

A sleepless night always ends.

†

It is better for your descendants to have something to brag about than for you to brag about your ancestors.

†

A soft heart makes a soft nighttime pillow.

†

You must learn the causes.

†

You are a good dishwasher if you dry them clean.

†

If employed, abstinence of anything, gets easier.

†

If you don't reach all of today's goals, you are still ahead if you didn't set any goals.

†

Your reputation is not the same as your character.

†

Trust.

†

Too many character flaws won't support a strong life.

†

Handle with care.

†

Truth is immortal.

†

No idea is bad because it's old and no idea is good because it's new.

†

Think.

†

You still say "What's for supper?"

†

Silence can be the loudest voice.

†

Be practical to avoid stumped toes.

†

Your heart has no wrinkles.

†

Business before pleasure.

†

Swearing is a habit.

†

Pride precedes a fall.

†

The snooze button serves no purpose but to delay.

†

Are you more history than future.

†

There is no rumor cemetery.

†

As a teacher you know more than others and others know more than you.

†

Manners pay off.

†

You are a man by life.

†

You measure your age by attitude, not years.

†

Be self-loyal.

†

Be yourself, not the tail on another dog.

†

You can have the last word in an argument by saying "Last word."

†

Thank you.

†

If you follow someone else, you must know his path.

†

Do your best.

†

Anticipate.

†

Do your homework, even after the wedding ceremony.

†

You conquer your faults one fault at a time.

†

You like books that make you think.

†

A big person rules his many smalls.

†

Bankers are leery of a person with a pick-up truck and horse trailer with matching colors.

†

A clock ticks louder on a sleepless night.

†

Think to be a leader.

†

Praise invigorates.

†

Don't tell jokes if you can't tell them effortlessly.

†

All offend: a fart, a fart inadequately disguised by a burnt match, and a fart joke.

†

To face your estranged friend or relative shrinks your differences.

†

You seldom aggravate strife or it grows bigger.

†

You've never seen a human with a halo.

†

To be merciful is to sparkle like a rainbow.

†

To get you must give.

†

The stars sparkle in silence, so can you.

†

Your habits take you down a path.

†

Quality is the best bargain.

†

The rich man practices thrift. That's why he's rich.

†

To honk your horn at another person only draws attention to you.

†

Speed bumps are for all.

†

You will always need a link to others.

†

Revenge is self-wounding.

†

Harping is a discordant tune.

†

Play life to the conclusion.

†

The devil is in the details.

†

Why aren't homemakers paid for their work? Because no one could afford them.

†

When driving a car, what is the condition you can stop on a railroad track? None.

†

Character is what you are in the dark, when nobody is watching.

†

When you are angry you become the victim, poor you, and you are at your weakest.

†

When you are mad or pout, after a while no one really cares.

†

Do you have a friend who is so crooked that when he dies the undertaker will have to screw him into the ground?

†

You don't care if she looks fat or thin or is rich or poor, but thin and rich is better.

†

If you think things can't get worse, you either drown or pull yourself above the waterline which brings peace.

†

You train to be a participant, not an observer.

†

Your child doesn't want to know about his/her father, but wants to know him.

†

You want to be the role model for your son that he needs, not the role model you think you should be.

†

There is an art to placing your children in the right place at the right time.

†

When you give someone a gift, the first recipient is you.

†

Rather than "Which way do you go," it is "The way you go."

†

Mistakes are a gift.

†

You adjourn the board of directors' meeting, then you decide what to do.

†

If your only tool is a hammer, then all your problems are the nails.

†

You know your child was growing up when he/she learned to say "no."

†

It's not what you know, but who you know.

†

You can't undo the sound of a bell after you ring it.

†

There is a very thin line between being opinionated, cynical, and mean.

†

Whoever angers you, controls you.

†

Rules without consequences are merely suggestions. Consequences applied inconsistently are called random acts of nature. It's hard to learn from consequences if you apply them inconsistently and randomly.

†

The only way you can have peace is to take it.

†

Life is all about your choices.

†

Desire is a marvelous feeling followed by love.

†

You can walk without going to someone.

†

After you have been married a while, you discover you are not married to "you," but to a completely different person.

†

You understand things only in relief.

†

The beauty of your life is in today.

†

If you have a vision, you can plan, and go forward.

†

Bought sense is better than borrowed sense.

†

The quest of revenge is control.

†

You pay for love with grief.

†

For a case of shingles disease, cover each bud with clear nail polish.

†

For night leg cramps, put a bar of soap (not Dove or Dial) under your bottom sheet. Replace in six weeks.

†

The complainer would rather vent than listen.

†

Life gets harder, the farther you go.

†

You can be stronger than you think you can be.

†

What you say "goes" and you say "go."

†

You try to be good except when it's to your advantage not to be good.

†

When you're right, that's all you get to be.

†

You must seize the opportunity of a lifetime during the lifetime of the opportunity.

†

It's not how you fall, but how you get up.

†

Bankers say, "You can't die now, you owe the bank."

†

When buying new shoes, try on the left foot in the early afternoon when your feet aren't swollen.

†

After others have let go, hold on.

†

Your victory over life is how many lives you touch.

†

Your net worth is living it and driving it.

†

You work hard rather than hardly working.

†

You reserve the right to have "selective hearing."

†

You become creative when you can't do anything else.

†

Applaud only when the symphony conductor turns to face the audience and don't stand up.

†

He works hard but not smart hard.

†

You try to not be "knee-walking drunk."

†

You know just how much sex to exhibit and still be dignified.

†

The language of love is dance and plenty of it.

†

You are happiest when your "To Do List" is short.

†

College is a learning curve for the parent and student.

†

If someone doesn't know how old you are, how old does that person think you are?

†

A man courts a woman until she's won and a woman wants to be won every day.

†

Death gives value to every day.

†

One of your best assets is knowing what the traffic will bear.

†

A little help to someone can make all the difference.

†

Your passion should cool before action.

†

Verbal self-defense is a law of nature.

†

Feelings are not facts.

†

Ambition that is ungovernable is noted.

†

History is a group of ironies.

†

You must remember to pull the little stickers off the bananas, lemons, and apples.

†

You don't fool your dentist if you don't floss.

†

When you were a child, Christmas never got here. Now that you are old, it comes twice a year.

†

Family is who you call when you are in trouble.

†

Men are as complex as women.

†

Outlaw power tools for your spouse.

†

Your work is the most rewarding if you already have money.

†

College teaches you how to get along with people.

†

Silence is so accurate.

†

Most of what you do is mundane. You live for the ten percent of life that is memorable.

†

When you know that your father is right, your son is now old enough to probably think you are wrong.

†

Know your children.

†

You are old enough to call your mother on your birthday and wish her a happy day.

†

Cut your credit card debt: quit charging, write down what you owe, ask for a lower interest rate, switch cards, exceed the minimum payment, save, and get other income.

†

Your soul has no age.

†

Life is life anywhere.

†

De-stress by breathing: inhale to a count of four, hold that breath for a count of seven, and then exhale to a count of eight.

†

An assessment comes with experience.

†

Don't spend time stalking a turtle.

†

Does your bathing suit bring out the best in body satisfaction?

†

It's not just about taking care of the planet. It's also about taking care of you.

†

The real beginning of happiness is gratitude.

†

Take the stairs.

†

You don't prepare the path for your child. You prepare your child for the path.

†

The United States flag should be displayed on the left from the viewing public.

†

There should be equal parts of giving and taking.

†

Heroes are made in an instant.

†

Do abstract or theory ideas interfere with thinking to confuse an issue?

†

Every consequence has a cause, so find out the cause to change the effect.

†

It's the crisis that distinguishes you and allows you to surpass others.

†

Be bigger than the temptation that is attempting to destroy you.

†

Taking revenge may change you, not them.

†

To have hope is the future.

†

Home is where the mother is.

†

You want to quit when the room is full of people.

†

You grew to your wisdom.

†

Give wisdom a chance.

†

Just finish.

For Writers

For Writers

Inspiration or Rejection

Writing is the making of meaning.

Writing is not the recording of meaning but its creation.

The act of putting one's thoughts on paper is an act of learning.

Inspiration comes from the actual writing.

With rejections, you don't know you have to be a good writer.

Fifty percent of writing is just showing up to write.

Aging improves your writing because life is a learning process. The longer you live the more aware you become.

Ideas abound everywhere and anywhere.

An idea is only the bait.

An idea comes to you and you write the thought down for fear of forgetting that one thought forever.

Writing immediately of an idea provides freshness.

If given writing topics only ten minutes before it's time to write an assigned essay, you relinquish your plans, and rely on your own inner sources.

Revising is an act of creation.

Your satisfaction in writing begins outwardly and ends inwardly.

Writing about your parents after they have died is like spending extra time with them.

The title of your next book may be in the index of your previous book.

When you write, see and study the pattern of words.

Common hurdles in writing are procrastination, writer's block, failure of a new project and the Internet confiscating all your time.

Writer's block is waiting to discover where you're going with your writing.

Writer's block is simply a fear or a feeling over being overwhelmed.

What is your preferred brand of pen?

On your computer you can write in any size font such as 8, 10, 12, 14 and even larger.

Do you begin writing a novel by writing the last sentence first?

Re-reading your manuscript should not be an embarrassment.

Re-reading enriches, but is not the same as the thrill of the first reading.

Is re-reading comforting?

Reading a good book insists that you pass it on to another person.

Are you an obsessive note taker?

You can edit anytime.

Writing by hand with a pencil or fountain pen is a tactile experience.

If you write it down, does your brain reject it?

Listen to orchestral music because music with lyrics can distract.

You can literally "cut and paste" if you write in longhand.

Writing is just organizing words.

Everyone has a story and lives it chapter by chapter.

Make a tape recording of you reading your writing and edit the passages that cause you to stumble.

You can print out chapters, arrange the pages on the floor and move sections around.

In writing fiction, a happy character is not good fiction.

Words are like people. They can be dull, stodgy, exuberant, exciting and most are the best company if you know them well.

A word can circulate orally for many generations or even centuries before it is included in a dictionary.

Does your writing make the reader laugh until his eyes are shut?

The rejection is like a forest fire that leaves debris to make the trees grow better.

✍

Word choice, metaphors, grammar and elements of style begin to develop along with increased sensitivity to nuances in language.

✍

A writing class is a rite of passage into the critical phase of learning.

✍

An idea is no one's property. Only the expression can be copyrighted.

✍

When a word eludes you, you lose track of time trying to find the word.

✍

Writing on a computer makes revision easier. Using a computer doesn't make you a better writer.

✍

Writing instruments such as pens and pencils have personalities of their own.

✍

Put pen or pencil to paper.

✍

When you write with a No. 2 pencil and make a mistake, you erase and all is forgiven.

✍

Writing with a pencil on a hard surface offers resistance as you feel the surface of the paper. You control the line by manipulating your hand.

✍

Have you ever regretted anything you've written?

✍

Swearing can be creative.

✍

You can't write hand gestures.

✍

Almost all peoples have invented and used a system for writing. Over two hundred are known.

You can decide yourself which font is good or bad and why.

Typographic terms: cap height (the height of the printing surface of a capital letter such as *H*; *x*- height (the height of the printing surface of a small letter such as *x*; serifs (a small terminal stroke at the end of the main stroke of a letter); sans serif (no small terminal stroke); ascender (part of the letter above the height of the letter as in *d* or *h*; kern (the part of the character which over-hangs the body as the top part of *f*; descender (part of the letter that extends below the foot of the letter as *y*); bold (very thick strokes); italic (letters that slope to the right); justification (lines with even margins on the left and/or right); leading (the spacing between lines of type); ligature (two of more letters joined as a single character as æ); font (the set of characters of the one size of the same typeface).

To write in cursive is joining the characters in a flowing, rounded manner. Cursive has been used from the 4th century B.C.

How do you know when to stop writing?

Paper for a published book is a medium to support and hold together the printed word.

Book paper should be aesthetic, withstand the rigors of being handled, and economical.

The book paper's shade and texture adds to the reader's impression.

Book paper needs to accept the printer's ink.

The look or feel of a paper is important.

Acid free paper is archival.

Parts of speech: nouns, pronouns, adjectives, adverbs, verbs, prepositions, conjunctions, and interjections.

English as a world language emerged from British Colonial power and United States economic power.

In *The Cambridge Encyclopedia* of 1.5 million letters, the most used letters are 1st–e, 2nd–a, 3rd–t, 4th–i, 5th–n.

Copying machines can produce heat to curl the paper.

Language can be coaxed into a telling that is never the point at the beginning.

You must have a keen awareness of your surroundings.

What you don't know, you can learn.

You are an insatiable reader.

Why are the possessive apostrophes vanishing?

Reading is the first step in writing.

You save the writings of your favorite writers.

It's a challenge to identify the books that fuel your passion to write.

You can name the books that speak to you.

When you buy a book for investment, a fine first edition is a must.

The bookseller's mantra is "condition, condition, condition."

To increase the value of your book, don't write in the book or put in a nameplate. Autograph but don't inscribe.

Dust jackets are critical to the value of a book. Don't cut off the price.

A writer's first book is most valuable because of the small number published.

Develop a collection of books that is greater than the sum of its parts.

Your collection of books requires proper classification and quarters.

Writing is mankind's most far reaching creation.

The origin of writing came from the need to record everyday life.

The power of writing comes from its flexibility.

Writing's power is its ability to move hearts and minds.

Writing is not essential to living.

To write you must work methodically.

The need to write is unexplainable.

The English language contains lots of "amps."

Writing is like being underwater, if you have gills you can breathe there.

Can your book be read out of sequence?

You think, so you write.

What you write is defined by who you are and your writing determines why you are.

Does music interfere with your writing rhythm?

Half the world's population has something to write about and doesn't; the other half has nothing to say and writes of it.

Writing a masterpiece begins with intent.

You are blessed with a storyteller's ear and a painter's eye for details.

Persistence pays.

Should you cross the threshold of a writing class?

A query letter is a business letter of selling yourself, your work, and if the work is complete or a work in progress.

Few publishers are interested in your writing if you are not a published author.

Publishers publish books based on the fact that few read, so they accept your writing if it is marketable.

Is there one brain floating around New York for all the New York publishers?

To get published you present yourself well.

To publish is a big game.

Find ways to get around publishing rules.

The joy of publishing comes from the writing, not the money.

Early in your writing career, were you advised to put it in the attic and pretend you had no talent, make photocopies for your family and friends, or publish?

As an alternate to rejection you can self-publish with control over all and the privilege of making mistakes.

To publish is to proclaim to the public.

You can't consider sales to determine if you are a good writer.

If you write and are unpublished, are you a writer?

A writer is one who writes.

Write tight.

Write the book, let it get cold, polish it.

It's not the amount of words but the meaning.

To write is to expose yourself to a voyeuristic public.

You seek to be heard without speaking a word.

You long to be immortal with your words.

To write a story loosens the imagination of the writer and the reader.

Einstein said, "Imagination is more important than knowledge."

Writing is another way to see.

You see using intuition, intellect, perception, observation, imagination, anticipation and expression.

Your writer's eye is more personal with the "I" if you learn to see.

A naïve seer thinks there is only one way to see. An experienced seer sees what he learns to see.

You write for yourself.

Surround yourself with talented people.

If you are a successful writer what you do for a living coincides with what you love and who you want to be.

Find a place to write.

Write with at least one thing of beauty in the room and you are never truly alone.

A teacup or mug is a must to make you sit down to write.

Writing is the process of revision and revision. You don't always know what you like until you are aware of what you don't like.

Guard your privacy.

You don't lose sight of feminine modesty which is about protecting hope and mystery. Respect for modesty makes a woman powerful.

You can write a "slow read."

It's a courageous act to halt a narrative which allows the reader to take time out.

Isn't it strange that there is so much writing and so little reading.

Dialogue in your story makes people come alive.

Read aloud your writing to find the rhythm.

Read aloud your writing when you are in different moods.

You could coin a new word such as "autoinspiramemoirbiographynoveljournal."

An autobiography is an account of your life written in the first person by you set apart from related forms of telling your life's story such as journals, personal essays and autobiographical novels.

An autobiography forces you to look at parts of your life you've tried to ignore. You write it for yourself so you won't miss the point.

There aren't enough pages to chronicle your life, so focus on the impact of events.

Autobiographies reveal shared eccentricities.

An autobiography doesn't have to move chronologically, but from triumph to tragedy to triumph.

Inspirational writing is to move the emotions or intellect of the reader either by divine guidance or suggestive opinions.

Everyone has a story to tell because nothing is so mundane that the event can't be woven into your memoir.

How willing are you to share with others your personal experiences in a memoir?

Do you want to leave a written record of your life?

Memoirs are written from memory to give a sense of continuity between generations.

Are you leading your life as a "memoir in progress?"

Memoirs reveal the tastes and character of the writer but focuses on outward events and people.

Memoirs have more than one version of the truth.

The biography is the story of a person's life written by another to record the actions and personality of the life that's lived.

The good biographer travels beyond the mere recording of facts.

The biographer's obligation is to give a close-up view of the person and with the writer's point of view because a person's life is more complex than just a listing.

The business of a biographer is to assure brevity, include the significant, and maintain his own freedom of spirit in creating one form of the truth.

Samuel Johnson said of a biography: "Which tell not how any
man became great, but how he was made happy;
not how he lost favour of this prince,
but how he became discontented with himself."

There is hardly a celebrated life left unrecorded.

A novel tells the story of a life not lived, but lived in fiction.

The attention to details—houses, furniture, appearances, presence, daily life, and ordinary dialogue—is typical of a novel.

In a novel describe the characters in pieces from the first, and with dialogue.

The intentions of the novelist may not be declared openly.

To not keep a journal is to lose the pulse by which you live.

Teenage girls keep diaries, women keep journals.

Journal writing insists that you focus on one thing rather than the eight or so thoughts roaming in your brain.

In your journal you write about issues by describing the event and your feelings, disregarding grammar and spelling.

John Quincy Adams: "A man's diary is a record in youth of his sentiments, in middle age of his actions, in old age of his reflections."

Your journal is talking to yourself, to posterity, and to anyone snooping in your room.

Your journal provides a sanctuary for your joys, pains and sufferings.

Journal writers are often high achievers and reflective.

Your journal writing helps deal with changes, keeps observation powers sharpened, and exercises inward feelings to outward events.

Journal writing is slower than speaking so writing of your feelings gives time to clarify.

In journaling you don't worry about privacy and your writing skills.

If you are a grownup you will criticize other's writing in a positive way.

Visualization is to put into form your mental images.

Your positive attitude aids the power of visualization.

To visualize you are not restricted by the concept of writing, yours or anyone else's.

All around you are gifts of visualization.

Your writing has value not only for you, but for others.

Creativity is to bring into being something that has its own identity.

Creativity begins with a first thought, then translates that first thought into secondary thoughts of reality. The second thoughts make the first thoughts visible and different from the masses.

You need a strong ego to create. Yet, to write you must set aside your ego to grow.

You want to write an interesting story, so you write your own.

The people who write of their life have better health.

You look for detail.

You have two skills: ability to use language and discipline.

You need to make the written word worthwhile.

A metaphor is using a word or phrase in a way that is different from its usual use.

A muse is any source of inspiration.

Wherever you are in your writing career you are further along than someone else and behind someone else.

Writing isn't as hard as you think, but you have to write a lot.

Write fast, polish later.

Avoid wordiness.

Avoid redundancy.

Do you write the way you talk?

An editor provides a fresh eye.

What is your ideal writing day?

What is your real writing day?

The textures of the world keep writers in touch with the world.

Your writing is compounded daily with continuity.

Stay connected to writing.

You end each writing session on a high point so you will know where to begin the next session.

A single writer's life can be lonely and having a child bringing an all consuming love outside the writer's mind can be quite powerful.

Having your family around demands discipline.

You try to have several projects progressing at one time.

The process of writing is all.

If you feel awful when you are not writing, you are obsessed.

You must believe that your writing makes a contribution to the world.

Elegance of form.

Rewrite: the more you write, the more you rewrite.

A sense of freshness.

You demand more of yourself.

How long did it take to write your book? Your reply is your age at that time.

To express yourself is a psychological high.

An outline takes away the discovery process.

An outline is a structure for rebelling and can be changed.

Writing is a journey of discovery.

When you put a thought on paper no one interrupts you and changes the subject.

You don't want to talk away any book you can write.

When you write it is like talking to one who understands you.

If you ever mature you will make one grand statement instead of so many little ones. That is, if you can sort it out.

A book is proof you were here.

Aimless scribbles of words, lines of words, and paragraphs connect to somewhere or nowhere.

When you write, you are at peace with your inner core.

You write, rewrite and rewrite and you are grateful for what you throw away.

The only title you have qualifying you to be a writer is that you are a person.

Writing lets you act out what you can't live out.

You look at women's writing in relationship to other women's writing, not to men's writing.

You need to finish your book in two year's time because if not when you finish you are not the same person.

Writing leads you to unexpected turns providing a sense of direction and developing of goals.

Better ideas appear if you correlate reading, thinking and writing.

You write because you must.

In a dictionary the stories are so short.

Write every day.

Does each compact sentence impart a short story?

The written word is greater than the spoken word because it reaches more.

You can collaborate by working willingly with any interested party.

Write and then get on with it.

You write for your times.

Your method is to work extremely hard in the right direction.

Success is due to hard work, simplifying, deciding, limiting, and giving up some things to stay focused.

Taking enough time to write is the key.

✍

Writing a book can be your volunteer work for your community.

✍

Encouragement is when someone says of your book, "I read your book and I haven't read a book in a long time when I've had to think."

✍

Attending an author's reading event is a shared time between author and reader.

✍

Most persons have one book in them.

✍

If another person can write a best seller, so can you, you think.

✍

Someone praised your early writings and praise is the winning knockout punch.

✍

Writers are compelled to write and fueled by what Einstein called, "The personal corruption of praise."

✍

Writers can't be overly praised.

✍

The world needs writers because on what will the motion pictures be based?

✍

Writing is what you do.

✍

In a small town writing is considered a craft. You want to rise above that definition.

✍

Being afraid is what causes bad writing.

✍

Doing too much research can keep you from writing.

✍

A good researcher must know how to use the libraries and Internet, know how to coax information out of people who don't want to talk, know no fear, and be part "blood hound."

Edit as you write.

Avoid "was, is, being."

Avoid "ly" words.

In editing: highlight in two colors every other line. If lines are all the same length, it's bad.

If you write one page a day, in 365 days you will have a book.

The shelf life of a paperback is three weeks before the cover is ripped off and sent back to the publisher.

The shelf life of a hardback is one year. If it doesn't sell the book is returned for credit.

In the bookstore inventory today, back to the publisher tomorrow.

If a book will sell five years down the road, it's timeless.

The best book titles have less than seven words.

If you can explain your book in one complete, concise declarative sentence it's probably good.

The contents page should tell you of its interior logic, what it's about, and where it's going.

While editing place your contents page on the refrigerator door for recognizing any problems.

The first sentence counts.

You don't have to limit yourself to short sentences.

Sow the seeds of curiosity.

The reader and you must vibrate together.

Provide quotation marks for phrases taken verbatim.

Doris Kearns Goodwin: "The writing of history is a rich process of building on the work of the past with the hope that others will build on what you have done."

Writing is a gift no one can take away from you.

What do you do to bring your work to completion?

"I" and "me" have a place in your writing language.

If you are a writer from a sheltered life, you can be daring because daringness comes from within.

The music of language.

A ghostwriter is a book doctor.

Members of a women's book club have in common a grass roots intellectual eagerness.

There is a system that weaves all your writing together.

It's difficult to analyze your own work, but you can critique other's work.

How grand to be a person whose every sentence conveys a significant meaning.

The only way to end writing a book is to begin another book.

You eventually die and your writing may be the measure of your life.

Litera Scripta Menet: Latin for the "written word remains."

Stories only happen to those who can tell them or write them.

The only free press is the one you own.

A long complex sentence is often rescued at the last with a verb.

Regardless of the number of pages in your book, your work is a long, continuous effort from the first word to the last word.

Anyone can Google a subject, but it's the writing that makes something.

There is no end in collecting books.

You know you are a book collector when you buy a book you know you'll never read.

Find your special voice.

Editing is to find the arc in the book.

Your books escort you for years.

You have to write to the depth of your heart and soul.

Use *archival pens to autograph a book.*

You have to sell your book.

After you write and publish, then you become a marketer.

Often if you add one more page to the book, the publisher will have to add sixteen more pages.

You write for personal satisfaction.

As you age you have a freedom to risk.

Your book is part of a continuum that lives after you.

There is a difference in language when writing or talking.

Polish a book.

You can write because you are afraid to be heard.

The difference between fiction and non-fiction is invention versus documentation.

Organize the research.

Reading liberates you.

You get more accomplished when by yourself.

You write because you have more to say.

Write to insist that the reader turn the page.

Your imagination tops your knowledge.

Collaboration breaks the aloneness and exposes you to new ideas.

You learn a lot from your book.

Stamina aids in writing.

Writing a book takes commitment and focus.

After writing a book, you need to get back into society.

A tape recorder is great as a memory tool, but depend on your notes.

Place notes at the end of the book to avoid being disruptive.

You are a captive of your writing.

You had the idea for your book about three years before you began writing it.

In your memoirs you wanted to revisit your youthful loss of innocence.

Writing is hard work.

You are inspired after you start writing.

You are pleased when you organize to write.

After publishing, you discard your notes.

You can write in longhand anywhere, anytime.

An autobiography attempts to explain how you became you.

Your memoir tells of an era and you.

Keep a journal of quotations that inspire you.

In examining other books, read the preface, contents, notes and index.

Your book is assertive in that you can tell others something.

Can you get back to your voice, your you?

✍

A television appearance to promote your book risks unscripted "ahhhs."

✍

Writing evolves from reading and hearing the rhythms.

✍

A slow thinker writes slowly.

✍

Enthusiasm about writing eventually leads to writing.

✍

You write about unimportant events.

✍

Word processors double your output.

✍

Book writing provides privacy and engagement giving you the best of both worlds.

✍

You like the research.

✍

A book is a primary means to convey ideas.

✍

Bookstores are better.

✍

A blinking cursor says to hurry.

✍

You need a clear voice to write.

✍

When you quit drinking while writing, you discover you have more time.

✍

An autobiography should be written near the end of your life.

✍

A memoir is a fragment with a theme.

✍

You write of searching for your identity within your marriage.

✍

There is no end in collecting books.

Acid laden paper is a "no-no."

Too many books, too little space.

An out-of-print book may be treasured by a later generation.

Digital books are limited because the technology changes so rapidly.

Writing the words is difficult, but reading the words is easy.

You write of nature and landscape to be an "outdoor writer," not an "indoor writer."

When you stop writing, you refuel.

English is a mixture of languages.

Hook children on reading when they are young.

The fate of a book is not linked to the newspaper.

Publishers with a fading readership can't rely on newspapers who have a fading readership.

An independent bookstore is a lonely outpost of civilization.

To have a good book needs a good audience.

The first time you re-read your book out loud, you know the work has been done. All you have to do is let it go.

The practice of observing yourself is the essence of writing.

There is no problem with book reading between consenting adults.

Promote your writing with a website.

Are you a writer spending your life telling the same story over and over?

The books in your personal library are your autobiography.

Book selling is progressive from the good to the best.

Most novelists if they write too much, become worse.

Strong talents usually exhaust themselves.

Are your book shelves so tall you have to use binoculars?

A book seller eventually doesn't have time to read all the books, so needs to find other readers.

Writing in your journal helps you connect with the writer inside of you.

Eavesdropping is a tool to inspire.

Take time to write but not too much.

Break your writing into small tasks.

You don't have to start writing at Chapter One.

At the end of all the "nos" is a "yes."

Creativity comes from anywhere—the newspaper, a conversation that says, "Pay attention to me, or else."

The index is the back door key.

Every rejection can be a stimulant.

Your personal library makes you an heir to the distant past.

Read books that make you think.

At bedtime, a "nightcap" book ends the day with enrichment.

Your writing habit is the avenue through which you move.

Be brief which requires thinking.

Write for academia in your own voice to avoid being boring.

To write for academia you must be competent.

You can learn to think by becoming a writer.

Practice writing is a discipline to be taken seriously.

Whatever is so long, save it for eternity.

Advice for how to publish is personal and ephemeral.

Approach your writing career like a holy calling.

Do you know someone who is a writer?

Is it a waste of time to practice writing in a workshop?

You are always writing in your mind.

Your goal is to publish something before you die.

You don't like being rejected, but your expectations were minimum and your patience maximum.

Why work hard to write something and then not share it.

Put your writing out there.

Let someone else decide if you are good enough to publish.

Don't pre-reject yourself.

After rejection, it takes self-forgiveness to begin again.

When did your clarion of truth occur?

You don't promise the world to write brilliantly, only that you will write.

It's only your fault you want to be a writer, not the world's fault.

Your desire for success is not the only reason to write; the desire must come from another place.

If you didn't write when you were nineteen years old, but wrote as you got older, your writing will only get better.

If the right person discovers your writing, the library shelves will clear for your writing.

How to publish books is often contradictory because there is really no one way, only many ways.

Begin with the love of writing, work hard in the right direction and let go of the results.

It takes courage to write, the true treasure is hidden inside you.

✍

If you aren't a writing genius, then inspire a writing genius.

✍

Easy reading books versus literary merit.

✍

Speed writing.

✍

Journaling is not a task for completion but provides an opportunity for self-expression, reflection and release.

✍

Journaling is recording the mundane events of your life and the important events.

✍

You recall.

✍

If you aren't educated as a writer you are embarking on an unaided journey of discovery.

✍

A writer is one who writes as an occupation.

✍

Are you an apprentice-writer?

✍

Are you a writer or an author?

✍

Writing involves a level of privacy and a much needed level of social engagement to join the best of two worlds.

✍

My actual writing day never equals my ideal writing day.

✍

You have to let go of the book to publish.

✍

The dust jacket should be clear, not faded, not torn and is left on although interior decorators take them off.

✍

Collaborators, co-authors, co-writers, writers-for-hire, book doctors, ghost writers aid in the story telling by writing every word, researching some words, fact checking, shaping text, and organizing an untidy manuscript.

The name on the front of the dust jacket is a matter of pride.

Another name on the front of the dust jacket is like having a co-star.

The collaborator's credit on the front of the dust jacket can be given as: "and," "with" or "as told by"—all in different font sizes than the author.

The left pages have even numbers, the right pages have odd numbers.

Pencil erasers aren't what they used to be.

The difference between typing on a computer and writing by hand is like walking on concrete versus strolling on grass.

In reading your journal you recall with fondness all the joys and the sorrows that tell you made it through the tough times.

Writing is a gift that you give yourself.

The advantages of joining a writing group: learning, critiquing, meeting people of like interests, writing and getting published.

A writing association is a celebration for the writing profession.

Writing is such hard work. Many give up before reaching their dream.

Words are weighty.

As a writer, you probably have more influence than you think.

Are hand-written notes a thing of the past?

A hand-written note is remembered for years whereas a phone call is a fleeting event.

A hand-written, personal letter stands out from all the bills received in the mail.

A hand-written letter has magic.

A short note can save time whereas a telephone call can be lengthy.

Receiving a hand-written letter can be calming, centering and bring friends closer.

Writing a letter of sympathy for the recipient can mean the difference between continued pain and beginning the healing process.

Hand-written calligraphy creates a special personality for your once-in-a-lifetime events.

Writing a formal hand-written reply to a formal invitation shows such good manners.

People with money have such good manners.

The number of pre-printed thank you notes in the stores doesn't take the place of a personal thank you note.

Announcements are more valid if they are not old news.

Parents need to write words of love and encouragement to their children when they are little and when they are grown.

A letter or note received is a tiny gesture that can forge a lasting bond.

Words touch your life.

Punctuation and spelling cause you more trouble except for grammar.

✍

Writing errors reflect on the writer's intelligence, knowledge and social standing.

✍

When several facts contradict each other, then find more than two and use the most prominent one.

✍

Be sure your punctuation works for you, not against you.

✍

When you write, the pauses, stresses, and inflections of your spoken voice must be represented by punctuation marks.

✍

Word order in spoken and written English is flexible.

✍

There was no need for punctuation before people began to write.

✍

The end of a sentence is noted by a terminal mark of punctuation, nine out of ten times with a period.

✍

"Which" is a non-restrictive clause or helps identify the subject.

✍

"That" is a restrictive clause.

✍

"Since" covers a time in the past.

✍

"Because" means for that reason.

✍

You choose a word, then strike it out.

✍

You can read a book before you gift it to someone.

✍

Writing is an escape.

✍

Write of what you know.

✍

A condolence letter, always hand written on good-quality white or cream paper, if you know the deceased and the bereaved is a personal friend, recall fond memories of the deceased; if you don't know the deceased and the bereaved is a personal friend, write to the friend of how he/she must be feeling.

Invisible ink is made with lemon juice, onion juice or milk. Dip a toothpick in the juice and write on hard-surfaced paper, dry, hold paper next to a hot lightbulb. For milk, use a toothpick, dry, rub with pencil shavings or fine ashes.

Just because short stories are shorter, they aren't easier.

At your reader's events, when people ask for advice–advise them to read.

Make a deal with yourself to write every day and honor that deal.

You come up with ideas by listening carefully and have a notebook.

Make your writing like a holy calling.

Do you really want to practice writing in a classroom?

You are always writing.

Are you a writer who picks a theme or are you one who has a theme happen to you?

You don't like being rejected.

Are your expectations too low?

Is your patience too high?

If your writing is beautiful, then share it.

Write from the heart and destiny will take over.

Make your writing noteworthy because your reader passes by your reading with a flip of the page.

✍

Your reason to write is not from the desire for success, but comes from another place that only you know.

✍

At any age the book shelves can be cleared to make room for your book.

✍

There are many ways.

✍

To describe emotions is difficult.

✍

Be loyal to your major theme.

✍

When you read your book aloud, be sure the it has a good sounding rhythm.

✍

Most writers could use a "story doctor."

✍

Every piece of trivia you put in a story may burden the reader.

✍

Make the detours short.

✍

Combine similar points to lessen interruption.

✍

To quote is to discover art.

✍

Drawings and charts clarify.

✍

It's hard to write an artful lead sentence that provokes curiosity, but you can try a scene, facts and plain speaking.

✍

Why would the reader want to read your book?

✍

The first letter in the first word is the lead into the lead.

✍

Place your published book in the proper location in your bookshelves.

Interior decorators place books as to color, height and length. But writers place their books carefully like placing guests at your dinner table.

Are your bookshelves located in your home, office or both?

Books pass from one generation to another.

Books are rectangular or square and easy to store or gift wrap.

Reading books is a convenient escape.

At your book autographing event, isn't it amazing to see so many people in one place who still like to read books.

When you are working on a book, it all seems wrong, but when published, you see the good.

Are your books between bookends?

Your library of books is a place to sense "people of words" around you.

Your library of your books is a collection of knowledge.

After you publish your book and you decide to read it, can you read it as others read it?

Give yourself to the motion of the book; analyze the structure and texture; recall the total form and reinterpret it at will.

For Writers Researching

For Writers Researching

Researching and Solving the World of Puzzles

Research is a diligent and systematic inquiry or investigation into a subject in order to discover facts or principles.

Research is the careful, patient study to find facts about a subject.

Key words to research: careful, patient, diligent, systematic, facts, principles, subject, inquiry and investigation.

Research is of value when accurate.

Research adds dimension to the story.

If researched adequately, the story may become the definitive on the subject.

All writing whether fiction or non-fiction begins with research not easily recognized as research:

What is the subject?

The subject may be already available or research leads to the subject.

Select a subject that seeks you.

What is the form?

Select the form by not starting and research other books on the subject.

Two requirements of a biographer: research and writing.

Something besides luck and hard work turns research into extraordinary writing which allows the reader to perceive the world in a new way.

Knowing why you write can carry you from intellectual passion to the physical energy of research to narrative mastery.

You may have a "defining moment" when you realize the subject is seeking you.

The rewards of research: one of life's greatest pleasures is to learn.

Teaching is performed in generosity and learning is accomplished with joy.

How many books have been written on the same subject?

Consult *Books in Print*, *Subject Guide to Books in Print*, *Publisher's Weekly*, and *Book Review Digest*.

Think about how someone will read your book. If it's logic or law it is read linear and if literary it is read at the pace it demands.

A practical problem in research can be solved by action.

Action occurs only in the world, not in books.

Question yourself as to whether the selection of the subject can be done and can you do it.

Consider the obstacles.

How much time will be involved in the research.

Use the *Chicago Manual of Style* for the latest methods.

You want to draw the reader into the mind and details of the subject.

Find a good book to use as your "role model" for your book.

Research for a "How To" book is in specifics and your recommendation is something worth doing. Use your personality throughout and know how it will be read.

A biography involves putting everything in place chronologically listing the birth, education, marriage, career and death. Much more is required to paint a word portrait of a life detailing the subject's driving force in life, conflict with himself, others and/or the world.

There is no right way, only your way.

When you feel that the subject is yours, then begin the actual research.

Consider how to house your research. There is no one proper system, only the one you install.

Assemble your material on notebook paper or legal/letter size paper and file in manila folders.

Label these folders with name of book because you may work on several books at one time.

Place your name on any research because it may get lost.

Transport files in a briefcase or box.

You can use long rolls of butcher paper, later cut into strips and mounted on walls.

Use large metal paper clips and expensive small paper clips because the inexpensive ones are too short.

In time the metal paper clips rust, so you can use plastic paper clips.

Bundle your material in string because rubber bands in time disintegrate.

If your research is housed in a museum, library or equivalent, the metal paper clips, staples and rubber bands will be removed.

You can begin filing your folders in filing boxes with lids, then advance to filing cabinets.

Prepare Contents for your files.

The smallest size binder clips conserve space.

Laptops are good because they have excellent memory devices.

Periodically make a back-up CD.

Use 4 x 6 or 3 x 5 index cards. The author, title, page number in the top left; key words or category in top right; summary of the source, direct quote with a "Q," further remarks on the subject in the body of the card; library, call number for the book and bibliography in lower right.

If you give a talk on how to research, remember that you may be considered an expert, but an expert is fifty miles from home with Power Point.

Avoid marking your research with a yellow highlighter because it fades quickly.

Use different colored pencils because when you try to remember some research point, sometimes the only clue you have is remembering the pencil's color.

Use Research Documentation Forms and attach to your research: date you obtained information,researcher's name, where you obtained the information, name of book, author publisher/city/date/page number, library reference number, and any notations.

Prepare Release Forms: We (I) hereby grant you, (your name) the author the rights to reproduce ___________ in your forthcoming book (name of your book). Credit to read:_____________. Name of publisher with information on your book such as size, limited edition, approximate pages, in English for North American distribution, date. Sign and send two copies, one for them and one copy to be returned to you.

Prepare Release Forms: I have been interviewed by (author's name) for use in a book (name of book). I agree that the author may use the material I have given her/him—oral, written or photographic—for publication in the book. I will not make any claims against the author for this use. I do not expect nor will I request any compensation for this material. Please indicate your preference of your name for acknowledgment in the book. Signed and dated, and return one copy.

For research trips take: paper, paper clips, scissors, stapler, binder, pencils, tape recorder, laptop, pens and whatever else you may need.

Determine where to research such as libraries, museums, art galleries, archives, government papers, and historical societies.

Learn the hours and floor plans of research sites.

Know what to research when visiting research sites.

Develop a friendly relationship with employees of research institutes.

Observe all the rules at research sites by writing a request, make an appointment, sign in at the appropriate desk, obtain an entry badge. You may be asked to deposit your driver's license at the desk. You may not be allowed to carry in your briefcase, purse, and pens. Only pencils may be used. The research institute may

do the photocopying. If not, bring coins for the photocopying machine or use a counter provided by the institute. If handling sensitive material you may be asked to wear white cotton gloves and to keep all material flat on the table. No food or drinks allowed. For security it is not unreasonable to be accompanied to the rest room area. As you leave your briefcase and purse may be inspected.

Use the Inter-Library Loan system at your public library.
Every book is available at a minimum cost.

Learn to research on the Internet.

Subscribe to an e-mail service because people respond quickly.

After so much research, the central theme appears.

Read for the subject.

Interview individuals.

Prepare for interviewing individuals. Know what questions to ask. If you can't get the answers in a reasonable amount of time, go to the next question.

When you interview other people and what they have achieved, you are awakened to your own potential to achieve.

Let you mind roam freely to think of the hidden pieces of the research puzzle.

When researching in books, read prefaces, indexes, contents, endnotes and bibliographies.

Learn to "speed read" to identify the main points.

Stay the course until you accumulate an enormous amount of information and the outside borders and inside pieces of the puzzle begin to emerge for a total picture.

When writing to someone for your research, use distinctive stationery. It attracts their attention. Make your point quickly. Provide a list of questions with space for answers. If they prefer, include your telephone number, fax number and e-mail address. Or that you can telephone them at a convenient time. You may have to "sweet talk" your way into prying information because they may fear exposure.

Remember that the life of an interviewee is not remembered in a straight line and memories are filtered through experiences, so piece together the memories.

Judge your interviewees if they are reliable, careful about facts and if you trust their conclusions. Then you are judged by how accurate you judge them.

Avoid doing all the talking. If not, the interview becomes your monologue.

Use your imagination and let your mind roam freely to think of the hidden research.

Walk the land.

Hire researchers who are familiar with your subject. These can be located at libraries, universities, county historical and genealogy societies.

Be careful what you research because you write of what you research.

Good research changes the reader's thinking. You take the reader down a new trail to accept new ideas. So you must provide the best reasons for rearranging the reader's thoughts.

How you spend your day is how you spend your life.

Are you overwhelmed with the research that is piling up in boxes, folders, and file cabinets?

Now is the time to question what to use. Simplify and condense because you want everything in your book to mean something.

Avoid the tendency to fall in love with your research so you can't part with the smallest detail.

After so much research, it's time to write.

A writer is not just a note taker, but one who writes.

It's not enough to want to win, to want to write, to want to publish, you have to want to prepare.

A book proposal is the first step in the actual writing of the book and allows you to make your claim either at the beginning or end of the book. Use your research to write chapter summaries. Whether you write the book proposal slow and clean or quick and dirty, just keep the ideas coming. You can always amend your book proposal. As you write the first chapter, missing pieces of research surface, and you research further.

The true learning of the principles of research doesn't precede practice, but follows.

Polish your research.

Research so that the book will stay in print for a year, have a universal quality and continue for years.

Your research will come together.

Research can lead you to your voice which can enchant you.

Research for your style which includes your own voice.

Be bold.

You can familiarize yourself with a location by "walking the land" many times.

Research is another adventure in your writing life.

When researching, keep in mind how a potential reader reads:
1) the title lures the reader,
2) the front matter commands the reader's time and why it should be read,
3) the contents with its list of illustrations gives a general sense of structure,
4) the chapters capture the pulse of the book,
5) the bibliography and notes tell the depth of your research,
6) an index provides reference to certain items.

Your research must be transitional meaning you link the events and/or topics together. This can be accomplished: 1) natural linkage using subdivisions, 2) by word or phrase-hook using the last sentence of a paragraph to begin the next topic in the next paragraph, 3) by questioning which usually is brief , 4) by time and place-shift which moves the action backward or forward.

Research provides background material for foreshadowing.

Research aids you by telling the reader what you are going to tell them, then you tell them, then you tell them exactly what you told them.

Research includes a dictionary and thesaurus.

Good research allows you to say what you mean.

The style and tone of your book depends on the thoroughness of your research.

Copyright is a form of property and each case is different. You consider the amount of material quoted relative to the length of the copyrighted work.

The copyright information can be obtained from the publisher or from the Search Division,

Register of Copyrights, Washington, DC.

Put the direct quote into your own words, remember only the ideas can be used.

When your book requires documentation and notes of your research, a style manual serves as a guide, but be consistent.

For Photographers

For Photographers

Getting Your Camera Out of the "Never Ready" Case

Photography means writing with light.

Two kinds of light: natural and artificial.

Types of lighting: front, back lighting and side lighting.

Front lighting is flat, back lighting gives depth to the image and side lighting gives more dimension.

Light has many moods.

To photograph is more than to reproduce, it is to transform an image into an abstraction of two dimensions.

In art, ability matters.

In buying your camera equipment, consider what interests you. Is it a hobby or a profession and how bulky is the camera?

Are you an amateur snapshooter or an experienced photographer?

It doesn't matter if you use an automatic camera or one with manual controls.

Use a real camera, not a cell phone camera.

Your camera takes pictures, as a photographer you make pictures.

Photography does not follow in the footsteps of painting, although the photographer is bound by the subject.

Does the photograph have a purpose?

Photography is arrested life.

Seeing is a selfish endeavor because you do it alone by speeding up, slowing down and backtracking.

Too much landscape overwhelms a person as the subject.

Keep the subject's head high in the frame.

Simplify the background.

Art is based on order.

Design is the equal of art.

Look for harsh shadows.

The photograph finisher can alter the color in a color print.

When photographing a one time event such as a wedding, work with a partner and synchronize your camera settings.

Be sure your negative is clean before printing.

Flesh tones are the best reference points.

Store your film and equipment with silica gel to absorb excess moisture.

If photographing outside and the day is humid and hot, to lessen the condensation on the camera lens take your camera outside for at least an hour before making the photograph.

Hold the camera steady.

If you don't have a tripod, you can place a bean bag on a solid surface to steady the camera.

You can sit down, bend your knees forward and use your knee as a tripod.

Look at photographs taken by the masters to see what makes a photograph great.

The essentials of a darkroom are the absence of light, electricity, hot and cold water. Your darkroom needs a dry side and a wet side.

Color photographs can fade, so periodically make black and white photographs of your family.

Few painters can avoid the issue of photography.

There is great complexity in light and dark.

The importance of the occasion.

Do you sign the photograph or the mat?

A portraitist attempts to reveal the individual behind the mask worn in public.

Airbrushing keeps the fantasy alive.

Does art begin in unhappiness?

If the world is falling apart, what keeps you photographing rocks?

You strive for a single masterpiece and consider the remainder of the exposures as trials.

Everyone has a story and photography tells that story.

There are no faces that are not interesting.

Photography is fun.

Your camera can be put away anytime and doesn't have to be fed or back washed.

To talk about photography is a waste of time, make exposures.

Don't record the sights of a city, but the faces of the city.

Are you a historian with a camera?

Do you understand the art of seeing?

A photography club's purpose is to support expressive photography.

Ansel Adams developed pre-visualization of your photographs which is seeing in your mind's eye the way the final print will look before you make the photograph.

Ansel Adams developed a Zone System for black and white photography. It is a combination of pre-visualization, film, exposure, film developing and printing. There are ten zones in the black and white photographic gray scale and each zone is one f/stop difference. The eighteen percent gray card is in Zone V.

Keep your camera battery charged at all times and keep an extra battery.

Keep images simple.

Have a center of interest.

The Rule of Thirds is dividing the format into vertical and horizontal thirds. The center of interest should be at one of the intersection points.

Place the center of interest off center.

Keep the horizon straight.

Get closer to the subject.

Look at the background.

Be aware of all the angles.

Use leading lines to direct the viewer's attention.

Frame the subject.

Include size indicators.

Focus.

Use your imagination.

Be aware of the light source.

The best times to photograph people are about 10 am or after 3 pm.

Avoid photographing adults too early in the day because their eyes can be puffy.

Don't try to pose children.

Put children in a relaxed setting where they are playing because they are unaware of the camera.

Encourage a child to strike his own pose which can reveal the wonderment of childhood.

When photographing your children, include yourself often in the images.

Use elements of scale with children.

Get on the child's eye level when photographing them.

You can't make too many photographs of your child.

Winning a nationwide contest or praise from a neighbor does not determine if you are a good photographer.

Whether a photograph is good or bad is a personal judgment.

In an exhibition, there's always one "best of show," one "worst of show" and all those in between.

Apply the ideas of leading lines, Rule of Thirds, size indicators, and good composition to end with good framing.

The frame on the photograph should not cast a shadow on the photograph.

Automatic cameras allow amateurs to declare photography as a favorite hobby.

It helps, but you don't need to know the inner workings of a camera, just how to make a good photograph.

Study and understand your camera's instruction manual.

Be sure to ask for your camera's instruction manual to be in English.

Which is the best camera? The one you can afford.

Never be ashamed of the type or age of your camera.

Don't be an accessory or gadget collector.

There are small, medium and large-format cameras.

The area of a small format camera is 24 mm wide x 36 mm long.

Medium format cameras produce square (2 1/4 x 2 1/4) or rectangular (6 x 4.5, 6 x 7, or 6 x 9) images.

Single lens reflex cameras (SLR) are more complex than point-and-shoot cameras.

SLR *cameras have lenses that can be removed and interchanged.*

Keep your lenses clean with a micro fiber lens cleaning cloth or a photographic lens tissue.

Never wipe the lens with your fingers or blow on the lens.

Try using Dust-off to clean your camera lens.

Start with a shutter speed of 1/125 to avoid camera shake.

Don't jab down the shutter release button, press it gently with an arched finger.

Hold your camera horizontally or vertically.

Think of your body as a tripod: feet slightly apart, keep the arm with the hand that supports the camera next to your body resting on your ribs as a brace.

Exhale before pressing the shutter release.

With a heavy telephoto lens and no tripod, use the side of a building or a tree or rest it on a chair, floor or fence post.

Load your film correctly into the camera.

International Standard Organization (ISO) numbers range from 6 to 6400.

Set the ISO number on your camera.

Shutter speeds determine how long light is allowed through the opened shutter to expose the film.

Fast shutter speeds capture moving subjects.

Focus on the most important part of your picture.

Focus on the eyes of the person.

Depth of field is how much of the picture from foreground to background will be in focus. Large apertures or f/stops are used to focus on the subject and blur the background. A small f/stop allows everything to be in focus.

Data Exchange (DX) films automatically presets the camera's exposure meter with the appropriate ISO.

With Automatic Exposure (AE) you slightly depress the shutter release button to activate a photocell that reads the light being reflected to your subject and triggers a microcomputer to adjust the lens opening and shutter speed for a correct exposure. Then fully depress the shutter release button for the exposure.

An Exposure Lock (EL) can override the AE. Re-aim the camera, push the Exposure Lock, then reframe the original scene, press the shutter release button to make the exposure.

To bracket an exposure, make two or more exposures over and under the correct exposure.

Be alert to very dark or very bright areas that influence the exposure meter.

A standard or normal lens covers an angle of view that is similar to what your eyes see.

A telephoto lens covers a smaller angle of view.

A wide-angle lens covers a wider angle of view.

The more the lens cost (not counting the advertising costs of the brand), the better the lens.

Be sure your camera and lens have warranties that are honored.

An AF (Auto Focus) lens has a setting for automatic (A) or manual (M).

Zoom lenses.

A flash is often used outdoors to eliminate harsh shadows.

A flash fired into an umbrella produces soft lighting when the umbrella is directed to the subject.

The flash and the camera must be synchronized so that the shutter is fully opened to expose the film when the flash is fired.

Red-eye reduction is when a series of quick pre-flashes or a continuous light from the flash causes the pupils to constrict before the actual exposure is made.

Be sure your fingers and all cords do not obstruct the lens or light meter.

Bounce the flash onto a white ceiling or a white wall for a soft, indirect illumination.

Check the film for the expiration date.

Storing film in the refrigerator or freezer may delay the expiration date, but is subject to some deterioration.

Types of film: color negative (print), color reversal (slide), and black and white.

Filters alter the light reaching the film to improve the image.

Filters that can be used with color films and black and white films: ultraviolet, polarizing and neutral density.

Use a polarizing filter with the sun at a ninety degree angle to your camera to maximize rich colors and avoid reflections and glare in the image.

A macro-shot is a close-up shot. Use a large aperture to blur the background.

When using a tripod, it's best to keep the front leg pointed in the same direction as the camera, so that you can stand between the two rear legs.

Carry all your gadgets in a single camera bag.

If buying used equipment, get a guarantee.

Keep your film cool and in low humidity areas.

Avoid placing your film in your luggage that is stored in an airplane's luggage compartment.

The airport x-ray machines can ruin high-speed films, ISO 400 and higher.

At the airport, put your film in a clear plastic bag and request hand inspection.

You can carry your film in a lead-lined polyester bag.

Airport x-rays are cumulative.

Film mailed may be exposed to x-ray.

Overseas governments often regulate taking cameras into facilities.

Foreign made cameras and equipment are subject to custom duty unless proof of purchase is shown.

Lens openings are usually fixed at one or two f/stops.

The built-in flash can be put on manual.

After learning the fundamentals, spontaneity brings clarity of vision.

Intuition aids expression.

A photograph leans a little over the edge if it has movement and energy.

Does the photograph awaken any interest and emotion?

Art in any form makes you feel less alone.

Pay attention to detail before the shutter is released.

Examine your feelings and thoughts about the subject, its visual attributes and how to organize such.

The essence of art may never be a definite formula.

Elements to consider: shape, texture, form (how it occupies space) and color.

Elements of design: dominant feature or center of interest, balance, proportion, rhythm, and perspective.

When to make the photograph?

The "decisive moment" is preceded by a fraction of a second before the decisive moment.

To capture the fraction of a second before the "decisive moment" you need quick reflexes, an exceptional eye for composition and the ability to expect the unexpected.

Feel and practice for the moment before the "decisive moment."

Freeze the moment.

Suspended time animation tends to generalize.

Time is the friend or enemy.

Light is the friend or enemy.

Challenge the traditions.

Pursue excellence.

The studio photographer plans the photograph carefully and exercises total control.

The photojournalist photographs life spontaneously.

Use tricks, a fast shutter speed and a strobe to photograph animals in a studio.

To make a still life photograph pay attention to detail, compare the objects for size and provide good lighting.

When photographing food have a second food item prepared, so the food stays fresh looking during the shoot.

Notice details before the shutter is released.

When using a studio, a front projection system can produce panoramic vistas.

Commercial photographers can have a team of assistants and the number varies. Listen to the team such as a casting director, art director, stylist, hairdresser, music director, prop director, wardrobe mistress, equipment manager and model builder—they must understand the photographer's needs and to almost second guess the problems.

To take the commercial photographer's studio on location, the photographer takes his mind-set to make the photograph he wants.

Once on location you need to be self-sufficient.

Arrange for archival storage of your negatives and prints.

The paparazzi is named for the 1960 movie *La Dolce Vita* irksome photographer character named Paparazzo.

A photographic essay is of an enriched single theme and composed of more than one photograph and more than one person (often an editor), and a design editor.

Every person can make photographs.

Today's generation is not documented by hand written letters but by photographs.

Learn to make Power Point presentations.

People gasp when a slide projector is bought out of the closet.

You can pursue photography at many levels.

A camera does not disqualify its user from being an artist, any more than a writer using a computer.

The camera doesn't make the artist.

Photography is just creating a picture.

Photography principles are liberating, not confining.

You need to know and recognize a good photograph.

The camera is an extension of yourself.

Wait for the best lighting.

Every item in a photograph is cemented to the whole.

To remove an unwanted item from a photograph, move the camera angle before you make the photograph.

In a still life, light is the key.

In a still life, use a matte spray on silver items to avoid reflection, move camera angle or use a light tent.

In a still life, fruit looks fresh if you apply a thin layer of mineral oil if the surface will absorb it or use a fine mist of water.

In a still life, use flash because hot floodlights will dry out and discolor fruit and vegetables and even melt ice cream.

A still life can't smile at you.

Position a person in a corner for the lighting effect.

To photograph jewelry use a light tent with a small depth of field. If photographing several pieces, put them on the same plane.

The great photography themes: the human condition, still life, portrait, nude, nature and war.

Photography can manipulate time. Speed it up or slow down and make things seen that are invisible to the eye.

Photojournalism is a "slice of life."

To retouch a negative, the subject's head should be as large as a dime.

Photojournalists tell a story and persuade.

Our appetite for photojournalism increases yearly.

The precision and beauty of a fine camera is not to be overlooked.

Some photographs are planned, some just happen.

Blurred backgrounds can emphasize movement.

Brace your camera if using a shutter speed of less than 1/3 second.

For a special effect, jiggle the camera with a slow shutter speed to reveal less detail.

Don't be afraid to experiment.

Use a camera you can handle easily.

Make lots of photographs.

Today photograph is an old story.

For existing light photography which is available light, use high speed film and a fast lens of f/2.8 or faster.

Vary the format.

Experiment by altering the color in subtle ways.

When learning photography just go to your back yard to make photographs. You don't have to travel great distances to learn.

Technical virtuosity.

Make enough photographs that you develop a theme and a passion for one particular subject such as faces, churches, trees, buildings, gardens, socially conscious images, or whatever.

The world is not as the camera sees it.

Does the contact sheet stand out by itself?

Documentary or street photography is associated with the 35 mm camera.

In extremely cold temperatures, your camera can freeze.

Some pictures seem to compose themselves.

Make images you need to make.

Ideas seem to be recycled.

Assemble your photographs into a book so they can speak together.

An archival scrapbook of photographs can take on a life beyond its original concept.

You can point to a great photograph easier than you can describe one.

A great photograph expresses what the photographer felt.

Use the best lens you can afford.

Photographs can peddle nostalgia.

In photographing older women, beauty is not defined by teenage girls.

Crop the negative space in a photograph.

What do shocking photographs contribute?

The art of illusion.

Are you making photographs for the printed page?

The first fixed image photograph was made in 1839 by Louis Jacques Mandé Daguerre.

William Henry Fox Talbot also claimed the invention about the same time.

The first woman photographer was Constance Talbot, wife of William Henry Fox Talbot who pioneered photography.

The greater the distance in time from the beginnings of photography in 1839, the more photography has come into its own as an art form.

Alfred Stieglitz (1864-1946) promoted photography as a fine art form.

Go beyond the masters.

Another breed of camera is the digital camera. They have the same goal as film cameras: to create a picture.

A Liquid Crystal Display (LCD) on the back of the digital camera displays the image to be recorded.

When photographing with your digital camera, keep both eyes open when looking through the LCD.

Digital cameras can be "point and shoot" or digital single lens reflex (DSLR).

If your cell phone has a camera, buy the one with the most pixels.

A pixel is a contraction of the term "picture element."

A digital image is composed of small, individual squares known as pixels.

Which is the best digital camera? The one you can afford that has the most pixels.

Before buying a digital camera, download from the Internet the manuals of your choices.

The cost of a digital camera depends on the maximum resolution determined by the number of pixels.

Resolution is the most important item in digital photography—how fine the detail and how sharp the image.

Resolution of digital cameras is indicted by numbers: the higher the number, the finer the resolution

The numbers are known as pixels often referred to as "ppi" or pixel per inch.

Minimum image quality is at least 640 x 480 pixels.

If a high resolution image requires 640 x 480 pixels and a low resolution image requires 320 x 240, you can make two low-resolution images for every high-resolution image.

Most digital cameras have an "on-off" switch for high or low resolution.

The higher the resolution, the fewer number of pictures you can make and the larger the image can be printed.

Outdoors, adjust the "white balance" of your camera to "cloudy" to get warmer and richer images.

The memory storage for digital cameras can be in formats such as Compact Flash (CF) which is the original memory card, Secure Digital (SD) which is very small with encryption capabilities, Multimedia which is the same size as SD with no encryption capabilities, Smart Media which is very thin, Memory Stick and XD. Memory storage is indicated by megabytes (MB).

Insert the storage system into the camera correctly.

When the memory stick or the equivalent is full, you can delete images or use another memory stick or equivalent.

With a digital camera, don't delete any images until you have revisited them days later.

The more you compress the pixels, the smaller the file but the more information your lose.

Digital images are quite large and are compressed into a form such as JPEG (Joint Photo Experts Group) which loses some of the quality.

Digital images can be saved in TIFF (Tagged Image File Format) where the original information is kept as is.

Digital images can be saved in RAW (or NEF) which compresses slightly, takes up more space and does not lose any information.

When showing the image on a computer the only thing that matters about the size is the pixel count.

A digital image can be edited on a computer with Adobe Photoshop (or the equivalent) which is the digital darkroom. The dots per inch (DPI) are how finely spaced the ink drops on the paper and control the print quality.

Computer workshops can alter color, crop and perform many finishing details.

A digital image can be printed by an online printing company, then mailed to you.

Be sure to back up your images on your computer hard drive or a Compact Disc (CD).

With the advent of digital photography some film types may be discontinued.

A steady flow of new methods can bring vitality to photography.

For Collectors

For Collectors

Or "I Can't Believe Daddy Collects China."

To collect is defined: To gather in one place; assemble; to gather things for a hobby; to call for and get money owed. Just ignore the last part of the definition of getting money owed, because you are giving out money.

Collecting is a good experience.

At any age it doesn't matter what you collect.

Asking you why you collect is like asking why do you breathe.

It's human behavior to accumulate, crave, classify, seek out, and hoard.

To collect is one of the greatest pleasures and adventures you can experience. If you haven't collected, you are missing the joy of finding a piece, bringing it into your life, living with it, and appreciating the piece everyday in a different way.

A true collector is there for the anticipation, the chase, and the satisfaction of possession.

Collecting is about passion which can be greater when long periods of time exist between looking, finding and acquiring.

Collecting is about order.

Related objects that you collect reinforce the others.

Have your head, heart and eye agree.

You can usually find a way to pay for an item in lay-a-way.

The rarer the item the longer the looking and the sweeter the pleasure in finding it.

Sometimes unrequited yearning is its own reward.

You don't own these things, you just care for them.

Do you have to worry about setting off security alarms?

Do you get too emotionally close to the items?

Collecting can start innocently.

Do you have an army of representatives who attend auctions and gallery sales?

You never finish collecting.

Is the collecting journey more interesting than the end?

You are just maintaining history as the caretakers.

Hobbies bring enjoyment, friendship, knowledge and relaxation and sometimes profit.

If your collection goes to the wrong hands, you might come back to haunt them.

The pleasure is in looking at the collection every day.

You buy things that add meaning to your collection without overpowering what you already have.

Train your eye.

Pursue formal study.

Always learn.

Be skeptical.

There are good collections everywhere in the world.

Is your collection an investment?

Less popular items are less expensive.

Rent a painting if you want to see if you like it.

Collecting posters should be in mint condition, but creases and small tears in the margins are acceptable; faded posters are not acceptable.

Antique furniture often is a better buy than modern reproductions.

Make sure antique furniture is in good condition: moves properly and stable, leaves flat and the same color, and know if it has been repaired.

Know the marks for porcelain, silver, pewter, ironstone, enamels, and any items with marks.

The cut-off date between antiques and non-antiques is 1830.

Find the rarest of the rare.

Quality jewelry should give pleasure for many years and many generations.

It's the smallest nuances that make the largest difference in quality.

Collecting can be dangerous because it's impulsive and addictive.

Collecting evolves.

Buy what you like. You are buying from your heart and head.

You ask, "Why collect?" Then you ask, "Why not?" Finally you ask, "What to do with what you collect?"

For better or worse, you live with everything you buy. Until death do you part.

Buy the item when you see it, because it may not be there later and in the future that item may be more important.

The experience of finding a great item for your collection isn't always handed to you on a silver plate, so search with an unbridled zeal and tenacious will.

Hone your collecting skills by focusing on a historical movement. Items with a historical perspective bring the items to life when you know how it was used, when it was used and how years ago it touched lives.

Shifting the collected item from its era to present day affects the meaning.

Explore a genre, consider broader applications, and build a bridge between your collection and other disciplines.

Pick a topical collection that is not too narrow or too broad such as collecting stamps based on the subject of the design rather than the country of origin.

It's helpful to have a focus for your collection which makes it more interesting. From the focus comes the passion.

Learn who is collecting what.

You acquire from around the world.

Do you ever sell your pieces?

Use your collection.

Provenance is comforting.

Can you replace an item that you sell?

The difference between a collector and an investor is that a collector wants the object more than he wants the money.

You usually build your collection on your feet and at your computer keyboard.

Your amount of collecting depends on the economy.

Even if you are "over the hill and testing your brakes," you can still collect.

There is "collective power."

Combine all the collections in the world, in the museums, private collections and your passion for your collection is as strong as others.

Keep your "steadiness of nerves."

You often want to own the complete set.

Lots of time the amount in your collection is enough.

Educate yourself at universities, museums and auction houses.

Collect primary source books on your collected items.

Court good dealers who can teach you quality and demands a thorough knowledge of the item.

Pay attention to the fine craftsmanship and detail.

The criteria for selecting one piece over another is boldness of shape, strength of decoration, surprises in the making, creativeness, and does it all work together.

All objects must pass the litmus test of quality.

Buy the best condition you can afford.

Mint condition holds its value and increases in value.

Collecting can make living a daily masterpiece.

The collecting bug can hit you unexpectedly.

Collecting is a kind of contagious virus, that once contracted, rarely leaves you. The virus can be dormant for a while, but usually reoccurs.

There can be a certain snobbery in collecting. Your collection is more important than another person's collection.

Your collection often reveals your personal characteristics.

Collecting has changed from feminine, capricious, child-like and frequently low-brow to include masculine, serious, mature, and high brow.

As you progress, you also acknowledge that what you also collect are debts.

Collectors die a rich person, not necessarily in financial terms, but having had a life full of improbable adventures and learning.

The financial side of collecting is never the motivation. The motivation is the attraction and to own something of beauty.

To look at a piece, you can go to a museum, but you'd rather own it. It's about possessing beauty.

Collect things that fit into your small or large space.

You know exactly what you are talking about when you make space for another item in your life and house.

There is an art to displaying your collection.

You want to live among your collections because they offer valid comfort and good memories.

Think of clever ways to house your collection.

The pieces ultimately tell you where they want to be in your collection.

Whatever you collect, make room for more of it.

Your collection is like leavened dough, it expands further and further.

It's difficult for four eyes to collect the same things.

It's difficult for a house to have two collections.

When you bring in a new object into your house, your spouse may say, "You didn't pay money for that?" When you sell it, your spouse will say, "You're not going to sell that, are you?"

Your spouse's interest in your collection gives you permission to collect.

When you make a list to look for item "X" you often find and buy item "Z."

It's fun to witness someone else's passion for his or her collection.

With e-bay, roadside flea markets, outdoor antique markets and garage sales, bargaining is part of the tradition. It is a dance of "wills and knowledge."

With e-bay, suddenly a huge amount of things appear from basements, attics and the rare becomes commonplace.

At roadside flea markets take a magnifying glass. Dress for a long, full day. You can take the children as a way they can learn to think, organize and absorb history.

Parents who like to collect, lead children to collect.

At outdoor antique markets, arrive before the doors open.

Estate sales have marked prices but the items sell cheaper at the end of the sale.

For garage sales, go to the more affluent neighborhoods.

What is your first memory of a collection?

You collect from a childhood memory.

Every item is a theater of memories.

Interesting stories surface about how, what, when and where you collect.

The story behind the collecting is valuable.

In collecting you meet others collecting with a similar passion, but with a different story of how they began.

You inherit something and become a collector by default. It's part of your family history.

You collect what is connected to your career.

A publisher collects books.

A railroad engineer collects miniature trains.

Using and sharing your collectibles is just as important as the collecting.

You collect because something is too much a part of your life to throw away. So you start a more extensive collection.

You enjoy having the items near you to hold and touch.

Collectors have a wide range of collection strategies.

As you collect, you become more selective.

To look at your collection refreshes your eyes.

You can collect more than one thing. One collection leads to another collection.

You are not collectors but rather acquirers, and live contentedly and inspired by them.

Collecting is like falling in love. It's a choice.

Collectors walk through rooms accessible only by narrow canals winding through mountainous tables of all shapes and sizes.

A collector can buy whole collections just to get one item.

Your inventory of your collection contains date, history, former owners, appearance, condition, and cost.

The monetary value of your collection can fall into the law of "supply and demand."

⌘

Your collection is part of the repertoire you have of "small escapes."

⌘

Collect something you can use.

⌘

To find bargains research and collect something that is not in high demand.

⌘

Each collection has one item that is the most dear, the most valued.

⌘

A passive collector is one who goes to shows and exhibitions, but has no direction and/or focus.

⌘

Just when you think you have seen it all, here comes a piece you've not known about or seen. These are the one of a kind rarities which go to private or eternal, public collections. It is fun to seek them out beforehand to keep them in the private domain.

⌘

Develop a keen eye. Learn to see.

⌘

Learn the advantages on the Internet such as "Pay Pal."

⌘

When you say, "Look what I found," you really mean you are capable of seeing and appreciating.

⌘

Today, antiques are everything from fine furniture to comic books. As long as someone values the item, you can collect it.

⌘

The Japanese have a term for an artistic, almost sentimental appreciation of the beauty of objects marked by chips, smudges, loose thread, by unabashed signs of wear and a human touch over the passage of time. It is *shibui*, a resonant little word that evokes the rustling of a grandmother's kimono as easily as it brings to mind the soothing warmth of a teacup clutched at dawn.

A collection needs space around it.

Do you have a favorite in your collection? Yes, all of them. They are your children.

Collecting comes from a love of something.

A love of the West may bring collecting Native American baskets.

A collection can be tied to a place you visited such as a collection of sea shells.

Your age is not a factor.

Consider the intrinsic value to future generations, if only your family.

There are an infinite variety of ways to put together your collection into broad categories or single items.

Limited display area.

Ephemera (small, inconsequential items of life) is collectible as proof of living.

The enemies of collecting paper: alum, inks, atmospheric conditions, light, temperature, dust, insects, and man (oil, sweat, tape, plastic bags, paper clips, staples and pins).

At first you collect greedily, then selectively.

With great passion you have collected, have a good sampling of mint condition pieces, and you must know that at some point you will dispose of the collection.

Place your collection where it can be seen by the public.

Provide a display case.

Mount a traveling exhibition.

Contact the motion picture industry if they have any use for your collection.

You are going to ride in a hearse to the final destination, but there won't be a U-Haul behind it containing your collection.

Is your attic or basement a repository for a collection?

Whether it's trash or treasure shouldn't diminish its value.

What makes a collection valuable: condition (mint or near mint), date (proves authenticity), names (a well-known name speaks for itself), signature (autograph collecting is an avocation all its own), and rarity (valuable because of its scarcity).

The final choice of what to collect remains with the collector, whatever piques your interest.

For Cooks

For Cooks
Or There's Nothing Like the Sound of Scraping Burnt Toast

Taste is like a muscle. Develop it.

Know what goes together by listening to your palate.

Hot and sweet, sour and savory.

Cooking for your family usually means one person doesn't like trying new things.

Replace regular black pepper with Szechuan peppercorns.

Add cloves or star anise to perfume rice.

We all eat!

Use the paper wrapper around stick of butter to grease a cake pan. You can save the paper in the freezer.

You don't invent a recipe. In some form, they are all borrowed and shared.

Do you want to be a pioneer woman and be among the first women to stop cooking?

Are you becoming a gourmet shopper instead of a gourmet cook?

Food fashions change through the years.

Okra is the key to good gumbo.

When boiling chicken pieces to skim off the scum, lay paper towels one at a time on top of the water, then discord. Repeat until scum is gone.

A person with a good appetite is one that will eat anything before it eats him.

You can eat off a casserole for a week.

Bay leaves are the key to a good pot roast.

Usually just one recipe in a recipe book pulls you to that recipe book.

Does anyone still cook?

Many people have a cookbook on their night stands.

One of the best things about the holidays is all the special foods.

The average American from Thanksgiving to New Year's Day gains about seven pounds.

Don't forget to keep your walking shoes ready.

Your turkey is ready when the inner thigh reaches 180 degrees F.

Anyone can cook.

Kid-fun recipes.

It is estimated that eighty percent of Americans eat whole grains less than once a day.

What is a whole grain? Whether the grain be wheat, rice, or corn…the level of processing of removing its outer layer is where the grain ceases to be whole.

Brown rice is healthier than white rice.

When using salt remember that a little goes a long way.

In the grocery store there are three aisles that have high fiber choices: bread, cereal and the rice and bean aisles.

Honey is nature's sweetener, but not for infants under one year of age.

With all the cookbooks, magazines and newspaper and television shows, there's no excuse for "I have no idea what to serve."

When planning a party menu: 1) respect your budget, 2) don't experiment with new recipes, 3) use seasonal fruit and vegetables, 4) prepare enough food, 5) simplify, 6) presentation.

French is the international language used by chefs and/or cooks.

Some recipes are simpler than others.

There should be one hot dish in a cocktail buffet.

Crudités are cold raw vegetables cut into small pieces.

A luncheon menu should be applicable to men or women, but not too heavy.

Laugh with your guests when your soufflé falls, the gelatin fails to mold and the bread burns.

Talking of your diet at a dinner table is the most boring subject.

The largest glass at the table setting is for water. The remainder glasses are for wines.

At the table if you are not drinking wine, turn your wine glass upside down to indicate to the waiter you are not having wine with your dinner.

Cut both ends off sweet potatoes before cooking to lessen the gaseousness.

Cook more than you need to fill your "brown bag" for tomorrow's lunch at work.

Pull the rack out of a hot oven before loading the cooking pan into the oven.

It's up to you if you use margarine or butter. Butter is better.

You realize that you are more important than food. Although you'd love a big slice of pizza, but you love yourself more.

Every cook should know how to make a thick, thin or medium cream sauce.

Keep an emergency shelf.

Cooking begins and ends with your family and friends.

Everyone likes hamburgers.

The best hamburger meat is beef: half chuck and half ground round.

Hamburgers are a good fit for everyone. Even vegetarians like veggie-burgers.

For fine crumbs grind graham crackers in food processors.

Bourbon balls will keep in a refrigerated air-tight container for months.

Soften ice cream and add your own ingredients.

Use kosher salt or sea salt for a better flavor.

Regular salt can be bitter tasting.

Iodinized salt contains sugar.

Fletcher "Old Dave" Davis from Athens, Texas is credited with introducing the hamburger with his first sales in the mid to late 1800s and at the Saint Louis World's Fair in 1904.

Hamburgers should be dark brown on the outside, right amount of pink on the inside.

Every restaurant has a hamburger on its menu.

Put cloves in beef vegetable soup.

Puree frozen fruit and add sugar to taste.

The delicate flavor of extra virgin olive oil is cooked away when heated to extremely high heat.

Freshness if the most important thing in spices.

Beautiful food presented beautifully.

A picnic basket: fresh fruit, cut fresh vegetables, salads if not loaded with mayonnaise, and crunchy *jicama* dusted with chili powder and lime juice.

Keep knives sharp by storing them in a wood block.

Using Eagle Brand Milk guarantees a perfect dessert recipe.

The scent of certain foods recalls memories of events.

To make ricotta, puree cottage cheese until smooth.

Don't ever refrigerate tomatoes.

Bananas can be frozen.

Gravy mix is flour, salt and pepper.

Good cooking.

It's easier cooking if your kitchen is organized.

Bake turkey with breast side down.

Preheat.

Bon Appétit.

Test and taste.

Foodies.

Cook for the next generation.

Consider cost.

Consider convenience.

Consider time in kitchen.

Good recipes versus bad recipes.

Menu planner.

Good cooks know what good food tastes like.

Choose great waters.

Music for dining.

Don't' be afraid of French cooking.

French sauces were originated to disguise the poor quality of meat.

Do you eat sparingly of the entree to save room for the dessert?

Making the ice cream mixture the day before will make it smoother and make more volume.

When making jelly, save jelly glasses from the last year for the following year.

Make jelly and jam with fruit that is slightly under ripe.

Coffee should be freshly ground and served immediately.

Tea is more delicate and steeps to perfection.

Use herbs with great discretion.

Your freezer is not for hoarding, but for continuous food thawing.

We are going to eat well, but differently than the Victorians.

Regional dishes.

One meal doesn't meet your nutritional requirements.

Lunch is determined by your breakfast.

Left-overs last as long as there is no protest.

Use only the best ingredients.

Seduction by chocolate.

An apron needs pockets.

A good recipe holds generations together.

If you don't cook, you don't make a mess in the kitchen.

If you don't cook, there is little in the house to eat, except store bought "cooked food."

It's a challenge to have everything you cook, be done at the same time.

When you burn a pan with sugary substance in it, put hot water in the pan or dish.

When you burn a pan with a flour mixture, put cold water in the pan or dish.

Greasy pans need very hot water with a dash of detergent, bring to a boil, let set a while, then scrub out burn.

If the pan is too badly burned, just throw away the pan.

Store perishables away from the refrigerator door because the temperature drops every time the door is opened.

The refrigerator should be maintained at 40 degrees F.

Eggs can be usable for a month if refrigerated and in their original containers.

Canned goods can be used for long periods of time if not exposed to extreme heat.

Canapés are bite size appetizers and come in all shapes.

Hors-d'oeuvres are appetizers.

Don't serve canapes and hors-d'oeuvres and then repeat the flavor in the entree.

Sandwiches made with day-old bread are the best.

Use scissors to remove bread crust.

Count the number of slices in a loaf of bread, divided by two for how many sandwiches.

Adopt an assembly line approach for making a large amount of sandwiches.

Cocktails before dinner are informal and they loosen your guests' tongues.

No more than forty-five minutes to an hour for cocktails before dinner.

Cereal can be stored for a year if in a cool, dry place and in a tightly closed container.

Food label: Open Dating is the use of a calendar instead of a code.

Food label: Sell-by tells the grocers when to remove the product from their shelves.

Food label: Best if Used By tells you when the product will have maximum freshness, flavor and texture...only a quality of product.

Food label: Expiration Date means to toss it if you haven't used it.

Food label: Guaranteed Fresh means perishable baked goods are edible beyond this date, but not fresh.

Coffee can be stored for two years if in a cool dark spot.

Toothpicks are helpful in serving, but the term itself is rather obnoxious.

Soup can be from white stock, brown stock, bouillon or consommé, broth, vegetable soup, cereal soup, chowders, cream soup.

Use little seasoning in soup while cooking, season when served.

To remove grease from hot soup, place a lettuce leaf in the hot soup. Remove when grease has been absorbed.

A meal should be nutritious, balanced and flavorfully tasty.

Ice cream and frozen desserts are best when frozen only three to four months.

Herbs and spices lose their potency after a year.

Bring everyday food out of the common.

Cook and test a new recipe before entertaining company.

Buy fish with bright, clear protruding eyes because dull and sunken eyes indicate it's not fresh.

A fresh fish will float in water.

To remove fish smell from your hands, rub with lemon juice, vinegar or salt before you wash your hands.

What is your first thought when you select a recipe?

Cook vegetables the shortest length of time according to age, size of vegetable and cooking method.

Meat: Prime is pen-fattened steer; Choice is the affluent shopper's choice; Good is nutritious but not as tender; Utility is good for sausage.

Certified Black Angus Beef is the finest.

One pound of boneless meat serves four.

Lean meat is often larded with thin strips (2 inch strips 1/4 inch thick) of salt pork or bacon with a dusting of herbs such as cloves or cinnamon.

We eat some of the same foods world-wide, only each country prepares them differently.

Keep all available juices from mild, cooked vegetables for soups.

Keep salad ingredients fresh, cold, crisp and dry.

Place lettuce in a wooden bowl, toss with a large wooden fork by gently lifting the lettuce four to six inches in the bowl, add oil to the seal the surface from oxygen, whirl the leaves slightly, and spoon on the dressing of your choice.
Then add any condiments of your choosing.

Don't wash the wooden salad bowl, rub dry.

Wash iceberg lettuce by removing the core by pushing it down and pull out with your hand. Hold the head upside down under running water. The pressure separates the leaves. Turn lettuce head upside down to drain. To add tomatoes to a lettuce salad dilutes the dressing. Use tomatoes to garnish the salad.

Slow oven is 250-325 degrees F.; moderate oven is 325-400 degrees F.; quick or hot oven is 400-450 degrees F.; very hot oven is 450-550 degrees F.

For the best desserts: pie is a runner-up to ice cream.

All the ingredients for making a pie crust should be as cold as possible.

Handle pie dough gently and as little as possible.

A cake should delight the eye.

In a cake: stir in a horizontal circular motion with a spoon; cream with the back of the spoon and side of bowl until smooth and creamy; beat with a rapid vertical circular motion to capture as much air as possible; whip with a flat wire egg whip for the egg white and a spiral wire whip for the cream; fold the lighter ingredient on the heavier ingredient using a spoon or a spatula and cut through the ingredients to the bottom with a downward stroke and place it on top.

Measure cake ingredients exactly, level and at room temperature.

Cup cakes can be baked in paper baking cups (one-third full) placed in a muffin tin.

To ice cup cakes, dip in a thin icing and swirl.

Start with the dish that has to cook the longest, then follow with the shortest cooking time.

As a newlywed your husband said of your first effort at chicken and dumplings, "It doesn't taste like my mother's." You replied, "It doesn't taste like my mother's either."

Can you hold a man's heart if his stomach growls?

He brings home the bacon, she cooks it or she brings home the bacon, he cooks it.

What's for supper?

Cleanse the palette.

Eating well is more than gourmet dining.

Eat healthy.

Make small, habitual improvements in changing eating habits.

One-half cup of cooked rice has only eighty-two calories and is almost sodium free.

Sharing recipes is a way to communicate.

Family reunions can be a way to share recipes.

Simple recipes leave time for other endeavors.

Quick and easy cooking is a talent.

You don't reveal that fixing dinner only took twenty minutes.

When sprinkling spices from the spice jar into a pan boiling on the stove, don't put the lid on the spice jar immediately in order to dry the moisture collected inside the jar.

Our ancestors whether German, Irish, European, Asian, or Hispanic brought their cooking style.

The Joy of Cooking is the best all-purpose cookbook.

Campfire cooking.

Present food as if a painting with texture, color, variety.

Food is precious.

Is any ingredient optional in a recipe?

The heat determines keeping the nutrients in the food.

One of the first lessons in learning to cook: face the stove.

Food cooked and brought to the table in an ideal state is called *á point* by the French.

Cooking seals in the natural juices, nourishes us, and pleases us.

High altitude cooking is an art itself.

Water boils quicker at high altitudes but it's not as hot.

Don't heat food in a plastic wrap in the microwave, because the plastic chemicals bleed into the food.

When buying food at the grocery store put your perishables together on the check-out conveyor belt so they will be sacked together. No need to alphabetize.

Can sizes:

Number 1-11 ounces, 1 1/3 cups

Number 1 1/2-16 ounces, 2 cups

Number 2-20 ounces, 2 1/2 cups

Number 2 1/2-28 ounces, 3 1/2 cups

Number 3-33 ounces, 4 cups

Number 10-106 ounces, 13 cups

Chefs are celebrities.

Which cooking school to attend?

Le Cordon Bleu means The Blue Ribbon.

Meal times should be pleasant hours of family unity and companionship.

Good food is a symbol of love.

The healthy family depends upon which foods are selected and prepared.

High temperatures, long cooking, and the incorporation of air can destroy nutrients.

Attractive table settings.

You need to dine rather than just eat.

Measure properly and most measurements are level.

A dash is less than 1/8 teaspoon.

Try to keep your dirty dishes to a minimum.

Four basic cooking methods: stew, fry, broil and bake.

The variation of the four basic cooking methods is the seasoning.

Seasoning brings out the flavor.

Fresh herbs should be used immediately.

You can shut off the heat and let the food stand for a while.

In seasoning, use small amounts. You can always add seasoning.

Garlic should never be overbearing.

A cookbook should not only provide recipes, but menu planning and how to serve.

Can you prepare thirty to forty meals without repeating?

Once you have used a recipe and it is received heartily, then the recipe is yours.

How much equipment do you need?

Purchase only good utensils because they can last a lifetime.

Utensils for a basic kitchen: sharp knives, meat and cooking thermometer, shredder, grater, slicer, measuring cups and spoons, stainless steel mixing bowls with handles, electric mixer and attachments, blender, casseroles, cooking pots and skillets with tight fitting lids.

There is no perfect cooking ware material so use which you prefer from glass, stainless steel, plastic, enamelware, cast iron, and Teflon.

The softer the margarine when cold, the more fatty acids it contains.

Food additives are being tested and until proven, should be avoided.

Read the fine print on can labels.

Leave the tea bags in the hot water just until the water turns dark. Left any longer the tannic acid which stains your teeth becomes stronger.

Have you forgotten how to cook?

Are we a nation of inexperienced cooks, but determined to learn.

Cookbooks for Cooking 101.

Anything goes for table settings such as tablecloths to place mats, only make it pretty.

The table centerpiece can be anything from flowers to your favorite piece of bric-a-brac.

Paper napkins and plastic flowers should be outlawed for indoor dining.

Lighted candlesticks are for nighttime dining only.

Mix your china patterns.

Toast the chef and the efforts.

Menu cards were reserved for formal dinners, but today menu cards are placed between two guests or in a special holder. It's a fun way to remember the event.

A cocktail party is really not a genuine "pay back."

A bartender should be hired when there are more than twenty-five guests.

Start cooking.

High temperature makes protein tough.

Salt sprinkled on surface of meat brings out juices.

Salt is added to stew or a meat soup to bring juices to the stock.

Meat has an internal temperature and an external temperature.

To keep meat juices in, brush lightly with oil.

In hot weather serve one hot dish and one chilled dish.

Salad ingredients must be free of moisture, then add the salad oil before adding lemon juice or vinegar. Lastly, add the seasoning.

The simplest dessert is fresh fruit, nuts or cheese and whole-grain crackers.

Don't let fruit stand in water too long and wash fruit rapidly to avoid loss of vitamins.

The batter for crepes should have the consistency of heavy cream and thinly coat a spoon.

For deviled eggs: for each yolk add 1 1/2 teaspoon each of mayonnaise, sour cream, French dressing, or soft butter mixed with a small amount of vinegar. Season with salt and pepper and/or dry mustard. You can spice it up with curry powder, sweet relish, Worcestershire sauce, cayenne or hot-pepper sauce.

To poach an egg: simmer 1-2 inches of water, stir the water to create a whirlpool, break egg in a saucer or small bowl, gently put egg into swirling water, cook 3-5 minutes, and remove with a pierced spoon.

To use an individual bud of garlic, pull it from the head. It will peel easily if you put the bud concave side down on a board, press with your hand or hit with a blunt instrument.

Only when nutrition is applied to meals can health be attained.

You want to want to cook.

Do you cook the same thing over and over?

Be sure to not get your recipes from the side of the family that can't cook or is culinary challenged.

Take notes when you cook and record on your recipe.

Publish a family cookbook.

It's a shame you can type recipes into your computer, but you can't cook.

Do you like your beef well done and actually cremated?

Burned food is because the cooks had rather talk and visit.

Supper is ready when the smoke alarm goes off.

Whose palate is your measure if a recipe is good or bad?

Tailgating tip: food should be ready about an hour or an hour and a half before the game starts to enjoy the food and have enough time to clean up before the kickoff.

Chop up left over Halloween candy and put in cookie dough instead of chocolate chips.

Where does food come from? The garden, forest or super market.

If the recipe calls for "1 cup sifted flour," sift before measuring. If it calls for "1 cup flour, sifted," sift afterwards.

When you shop at the grocery store, why is there always one broken egg in a package of twelve and one rotten strawberry in the bottom of a package of strawberries?

The food you crave can become your poison.

There are 8,760 hours in a 365 day year and you spend approximately 1,095 hours a year eating.

Do they make double-wide dishwashers for the home?

A cake from a mix may not be as good as one from scratch, but it's easier.

There was a migration from the stove after World War II.

If you celebrate your golden wedding anniversary, a woman may have cooked approximately 54,750 meals.

For Travelers

For Travelers

Or Never Judge a Hotel By Its Lobby

Where to go?

Plan your budget, then double it.

Bring your identification, passport and copies of each.

If you leave the United States, you will need your passport.

For obtaining a passport quickly, go to the passport office in person.

Everyone needs a passport and you can apply in person for your first passport.

Passports are good for ten years if you are over eighteen years old, for five years if you are under seventeen.

In case of a stolen or lost passport always carry a copy of your passport when traveling out of the country.

Prepare your house to avoid burglaries.

Make two copies of your itinerary.

Leave one copy of your itinerary with someone.

Plan your trip even to where you can check your e-mail.

When you leave, be sure all the animals are out of your house.

Protect your home: use a timer or photo electric cell that turns on lights at dusk.

Protect your home: use a motion detector light outside.

Protect your home: leave a radio or television on to give a lived-in appearance.

Protect your home: close and lock garage doors.

Protect your home: secure points of entry.

Protect your home: use a monitored security system.

Protect your home: lock up tools such as a ladder that a burglar can use.

Protect your home: trim shrubbery especially under windows.

Protect your home: install new locks if in a new home or apartment.

Keep your pet in the car in a harness attached to a seat belt in case you stop suddenly.

Feed your pet three to four hours before you depart.

Bring plenty of water for your pet.

Bring the cat in a carrying box and the cat's litter box.

Don't ever leave your pet unattended in the car, regardless of how ventilated.

Avoid the "tourist traps."

The travel industry is volatile.

How would you travel on your "dream trip?"

The average tourist looks at the Grand Canyon for seventeen minutes.

Does saving money really save time on a trip?

Your airfare depends on class of service such as coach or first class, fare category as to how many days, staying over a Saturday night, low or high season, purchased online or from a travel agent, peak times, and when overall demand for tickets is high or low.

Do you chance waiting for the airline ticket sale?

Stand-by airline tickets are not discounted.

Nothing is worse than waiting at the airport for your baggage to arrive and it doesn't arrive on the conveyor belt.

Check with the airline for their policy on checking baggage such as number allowed, weight, charge and size. The policies change frequently.

If your luggage is lost and you need to replenish some supplies for an immediate engagement, be sure to keep receipts. Reimbursement will depend on the airline's goodwill.

To receive payment for lost luggage, the amount is $2,500 but you must produce receipts.

Plan as far in advance as you can for the best airfares.

You can always fly "Open Jaw" when you fly into one city, return from another city by traveling between the two cities by land or sea.

Airport VIP lounges may be offered on one-day or monthly passes.

Checked strollers and infant seats are not charged an airline baggage fee.

Best time of day to shop domestic airline tickets is Tuesday afternoon.

Airline flights are less full in the mornings,
Tuesdays, Wednesdays or Saturdays.

The fall is the slowest airline season.

The key to getting a cheap airfare is research.

When you see the best airline deal, take it.

Put as many items as you can in your carry-on bag that goes through the security screening.

When traveling with someone, it's comfortable to each have aisle seats.

The safest seats on an airplane are aisle seats over the wing.

To minimize ear pain when flying chew gum or hold your nose and blow.

Southwest Airlines seating is "first come, first serve."

The odds of finding an open middle seat are better at the back of the plane.

On an airplane the last row of seats do not recline.

Emergency row seats have more leg room but you can't sit in them unless you can operate the emergency door.

An airfare consolidator purchases discounted tickets from the airline and guarantees a volume. He marks up the price from wholesale or receives a rebate on the retail cost.

A travel agent earns his fees from the client, and commissions from the airline and tour operators.

If you travel frequently, it may be worth the annual fee to belong to an airline lounge.

Use your frequent flyer miles.

It takes time to use the Internet travel sites: Orbitz.com, Expedia.com, Travelocity.com, Hotwire.com, Tripadvisor.com, Cheaptickets.com, Overstock.com, Traveltactics.com, Site59.com, 11thhourvacations.com, Concierge.com, Lastminutetravel.com, Smarterliving.com. Consolidators: Flights.com. Luxurylin.com for the elegant vacationer. In time more websites will be added or deleted.

See the museums, cathedrals, statues and galleries, but don't forget the people, the sights and sounds.

Discover the overlooked gems.

When in a city that is unfamiliar, the quickest way to find an all-night drugstore is to call the police.

Be aware that hotel thieves often converse with a person on the elevator, then get off on the same floor, wait until you open your door, then barge into your room.

Put your name, office address, office telephone number on your luggage tag, not your home information.

If you have less than two hundred miles to travel, it's easier to drive rather than fly.

The best place to eat is not always the truck stop, because their first priority is a large parking lot.

When you put the tire to the pavement, you are on a road trip.

Check the local tradition for tipping the maitre d', waiter, sommelier, cloakroom, doorman.

Don't travel with your fine jewelry, streamline your wallet, tell someone of your plans, inventory your items, wear a wedding ring, and have single bills ready to tip.

Do you really want to travel for a year after raising the children and before old age?

How hard is it to break away to be gone from "home" for a year?

To take a year long trip requires freeing up your income to spend it on the trip, planning, and actually leaving the house.

When traveling pick a clothes color scheme and build around it. Don't take anything that can't be mixed or matched.

Traveling triggers excitement.

Your essence gets left behind.

Foul weather tests a vacation.

You are grateful for what you had enjoyed and greedy for what you hadn't.

Money is fleeting.

When you car breaks down, get the car out of the line of traffic, turn on your emergency flasher lights, tie a white cloth to the driver's door handle, raise the hood and stay in the car. Or call AAA.

Check for overrated and disappointing sights.

Hotels expect business travelers to be insensitive to price.

Often great hotel rates are not commissioned for the travel agent.

If location is important, do you know where it is located on a map?

Before checking in, ask the bellman which are the best rooms. He will appreciate the extra gratuity.

A hotel consolidator buys blocks of hotel rooms at volume discounts in cities each night.

Ask for different hotel rates for American Association of Retired People (AARP), American Automobile Association (AAA), corporate or any other special rate.

Use your hotel points. They are earned exclusively in direct proportion to the dollars you spend.

Why do you travel in the first place?

Before you sign up for car rental insurance, know what coverage you have on your personal automobile.

To rent a car in one city and drop off in another city usually costs $100 or more unless the company needs to move the car from one location to another. Be sure to ask.

Be sure to ask if the car rental company is an off-airport location.

Ask for AAA, AARP car rental rates.

Be sure to ask about returning your rental car with a full tank of gasoline.

Check to see if the rental car is "unlimited mileage."

Smart car rental drivers join "Express Pickup."

Use "Affinity Cards" which is a credit card that pays back the cardholder with a reward of frequent flier miles or hotel points, for an annual fee.

In writing a complaint letter: express the good and the bad, document the facts, write within a short time after the incident, write on a word-processor with attractive stationery and envelope, personalize the event, be brief, be business-like, send any documentation, request reasonable compensation, give a deadline, and keep a copy.

You may not find spaghetti and meatballs in Italy because it's an American dish.

Avoid the dangerous terrorist areas.

Learn just a few key words of a foreign language.

Ten rules for air travel: it's difficult and expensive; book smartly by choosing the best flights at the best time; plan for trouble; have fun but learn something; find perks such as airport clubs with day passes; be loyal to one airline to enjoy collecting miles; check only what you can do without; upgrade when you can; ask everyone nicely; and be kind to your fellow travelers.

If you speak English slowly and louder, the foreign language person will still not understand you.

You won't find the local people wearing their regional traditional costume.

Take the road less traveled.

Watch some local television.

Rent an apartment or villa in a foreign land.

Stroll through a local neighborhood.

Have a long candlelight dinner anywhere.

Picnic.

Delete duplicates because once you've seen a couple of cathedrals, you've seen them all.

Day trips add variety.

If you are traveling with a group, split up.

Assume that you will return someday to see the sights you missed.

Ten days is a good length of time to be gone from home.

Try spontaneity.

National tourists boards will send you an envelope full of brochures.

Log on to the Internet for information.

Choose a guidebook that fits your personality.

When is the best time to travel? When you can arrange the vacation time.

The climate varies from country to country.

Do you avoid the popular tourist season?

Consider the "high season" and "low season" and the in-between known as the "shoulder season."

Consider when the holiday and festival seasons begin and end.

Make reservations for your rooms as soon as possible.

Do you get in the mood before the trip by reading books, seeing films or attending classes?

Traveling with your young children means you see the zoos, travel slower, and their minds are opened to the diversity of the world's people and culture.

Traveling with people over sixty years of age is beneficial because most foreign countries treat seniors with great respect.

Disability is not dealt with in foreign countries as nicely as in the United States, but they are gaining on it.

Students often are entitled to a discount if you show your ID card.

Your travel agent can be your friend or foe.

Travel agents get paid by the hotel, airline, and tour company, so be leery of their booking you for the best commission.

Do your homework with a travel agent.

Escorted tours free you from deciphering everything.

For an escorted tour find out the cancellation policy, how tight is the schedule, how big is the group, and what is included.

Take an escorted specialty tour such as hiking, biking, art history, opera and cooking.

For your peace of mind, if you travel alone reserve a few hotels and restaurants before your leave.

Airfare is what the market will bear.

Most foreign countries partner with American Airlines.

The bulkhead seats in the front row have the most leg room, but you have to store your carry-ons in the overhead bin.

It's hard to see the in-flight movie from the bulkhead seats.

Don't leave anything unattended in the airport.

Emergency row seats have more room, but your carry-ons are put in the overhead bin.

Learn to tell time by the Military Time.

Master the city's rail or subway system.

Most train schedules use native names for the cities: Athens is Athinai, Colgone is Köln.

Take overnight train rides to save on time while you sleep on uncomfortable beds.

Check on the types of Train Passes.

Calculate travel time in miles and/or kilometers.
One kilometer equal .6 miles.

There are ATM machines in most train stations and airports.

Be aware of pickpockets everywhere.

If you rent a car, are you prepared to drive on the left side?

Make scenic drives.

A rental stick shift automobile is cheaper than automatic shift.

Inspect the rental car before your drive away.

Make photographs of the rental car before you drive away.

Look for ways to avoid long lines.

Walk a lot.

Stay in a room with king beds rather than two beds because fewer sheets to wash means a savings to you.

Wash a few things in the room sink every night, roll them in towels to absorb the moisture, lay on a radiator or a heated towel rack.

Eat heartily if breakfast is included in the price.

Eat at the finest restaurants at lunch, rather than at dinner.

Check the restaurant bill before adding a gratuity.

Check for free nights at museums.

Save on your time.

Skip buying the souvenirs to save money.

Certain credit cards are almost universally accepted.

Be sure it's safe to drink the local water.

Pack light. You usually keep wearing what is on top in the suitcase.

It's okay, usually, if a hotel wants to keep your passport overnight. You can tell them you need your passport quickly to exchange money at the bank.

If you lose your passport, go directly to the American embassy and bring all your ID.

You can bring back any amount of goods into the United States, but only so much duty free.

Head to the local pharmacy if you get sick.

Buy only the travel insurance that you need.

Take enough of your prescription medicine for the trip plus an week extra.

Keep prescriptions in original containers.

You will need Pepto-Bismol, Imodium, and Kaopectate for indigestion and diarrhea; Dramamine for air sickness; a decongestant to take before your flight to discourage ear-popping.

Carry-on luggage for the airplane doesn't mean all the contents of your house.

Leave space in your luggage for purchases on the trip.

Your clothes in your luggage fluff up after a while.

For security regulations, each carry on liquid bottle should be no more than three ounces.

For security regulations, put all liquids in plastic bottles and place inside a plastic quart bag.

Half of a tennis ball makes a good sink stopper.

Bring only battery operated electrical equipment and extra batteries.

At home put a vacation hold on your mail and newspapers.

Reconfirm any reservations.

If on an extended trip, ask a neighbor to start your car once a week.

Make arrangement for a shuttle service or a friend to take you to the airport.

Airport garages are expensive.

A hotel is just a place to lay your head.

Does the early bird get the hot shower?

That second commode is a *bidet* which does a better job of cleaning.

If the time difference is great, book your hotel room for the previous night, so you can have it available when you arrive.

If your flight leaves late in the day, book an extra hotel room for that night because check-out time is usually at noon.

International hotel chains usually offer a nice level of amenities and services.

For staying in a "Farm Stay" take your chances. Some are luxurious, some are close to sleeping with the cows.

Hostels are often far from the center of town, on a per-person rate and baths are shared.

Fine dining can last two to three hours.

The interior decor of a fine restaurant often looks worn out.

Water at a table is not a given. Ask for tap, fizzy or non-fizzy.

Ice in your drinks is not a given in most countries.

Waiters don't announce their name, they simply wait on you.

Your salad comes at the end of the meal.

Try not to eat at American fast food restaurants in foreign countries just because you are in a hurry and hungry.

Make lots of photographs.

A mid-day nap.

Monday closings?

To enjoy a museum: visit it twice, split up the group, it's your option to take a guided tour or the audio tour, concentrate on the masterpieces and look at what you like.

City sightseeing bus tours give you an overview.

Are you obligated to see everything just because it's famous?

Pace yourself.

Vary your sightseeing.

Take a break when everything looks the same.

Get off the beaten track.

Know your camera and practice making photographs.

You will probably make it home before your mailed postcard arrives.

The language barrier can be lessened with pantomime.

You must be American because you only speak one language.

Let the locals be the guide as to how to act and when to touch a person.

Keep important papers and money in a money belt that is worn at all times.

Put the day's spending money in your wallet or purse.

Ladies, carry your purse strap across your chest, not on your shoulder.

Keep walking if children, beggars or gypsies approach you.

The guide on a guided tour usually gets a "kick-back" from the recommended store or restaurant.

Don't flash your valuables.

Make copies of the United States phone numbers to report stolen or lost credit cards.

Terrorist attacks are a random act that can happen anywhere.

Shop for items that define the local culture.

The main shopping street offers great window shopping and great prices.

Shop the street markets for the best haggling and best prices.

Take your time to always haggle, don't appear too interested, and try walking away.

Know the Value Added Tax (VAT) refund minimum.

Ship all the breakables to your home.

If you need room in your luggage, ship your dirty laundry home.

Consult the clothing size charts because sizes vary among countries and manufacturers.

To avoid hackers when using computers and Wi-Fi networks in a hotel room or lobby, café and airport use safeguards such as a strong password, a dedicated e-mail account for use on the road, remove traces of your browsing or set up a Virtual Private Network (VPN).

Travel light.

Your luxuries or comforts are dispensable and hindrances.

The hardships and mishaps of travel become the basis for stories to tell your friends and family.

Anticipation, planning and reading are part of the travel.

Bring extra glasses, prescriptions, and hearing aid batteries.

Some sites interest you, some don't.

Get ready for retirement and travel.

You will see history you don't have to remember, but history you can't forget.

Accuracy is everything to the airplane pilot.

When you are a guest at someone's house, leave everything in place as you found it.

When you are a house guest, make your bed, hang up your towels, and put your dishes in the dishwasher.

It's pleasant, as an older person, to travel with people in their twenties because they sleep late and don't want to start the day until about 10 am.

Have you been everywhere?

Experience history.

Travel with an escorted tour if you want to save money, avoid hassles, go to a special event, to travel to less-developed countries, pursue a special interest and make new friends.

The year 2009 marked the fortieth anniversary of the film *If It's Tuesday, This Must be Belgium.*

The German Autobahn has begun applying speed limits.

Do you need to travel with a suitcase for your medicine?

Traveling to the most remote unspoiled places restores your soul.

If you belong to American Automobile Association, use their TripTik to plan your automobile travel route.

The automobile invention is one of a kind, but the network of highways gave the automobile some place to go.

The best camping tent should be made of nylon, have good cross ventilation, mesh openings, windows that keep out the storms, have lap-felled seams, and at least eighty square feet for a family of four.

Two types of vacations: discovering something new and exciting or a laid-back time.

Guide books are of two types: ones that provide essays describing the mood and atmosphere and ones that provide specifics.

U. S. Route 66, accepted as the law of the land in 1926, did not follow earlier trade routes established by earlier generations, but went from Chicago, Illinois to Santa Monica, California.

Do you take several small trips or one grand trip for a year focusing on just what you want to do.

The grand trip will take so much planning that you probably won't want to do it but once.

To save gas while traveling, don't idle the car.

A little bit of travel for everyone.

Escape.

For Retirees

For Retirees

Or It's Okay To Be Young and Poor, But You Don't Want To Be Old and Poor

Retirement is when your proud days of yesterday's accomplishments meet the hopes and dreams of tomorrow.

✦

When you retire, retire into something else.

✦

Your husband can retire anytime he has some place to go between 8 am and 5 pm.

✦

When your husband retires, the wife's life stays the same.

✦

As you age you need to not let your idiosyncrasies take control.

✦

When you are retirement age, no one takes you hostage or kidnaps you.

✦

You are not expected to run anywhere.

✦

Your death ends your life, but not your relationship.

✦

In retirement, gravity does not sleep.

✦

When someone asks, "Are you retired?" Answer, "No, I'm too busy retiring."

✦

Are you at the age where there is very little that interests you after 10 pm.

✦

You can't learn anything else the hard way.

In your old age you can do the things you did in your youth, but you pay the price.

Aging is a lot of output, but little gain.

At your age you wonder how good are you supposed to look.

Supper is at 4:30 pm.

You inherit the body of your youth.

Your gray hair and gray matter give you double power; add enthusiasm and you triple your power.

You don't have enough time left in your life to spend with your enemies, you want to spend the time with your friends.

If invited to a party with young guests, don't arrive early.

In retirement you become a long term optimist and at the same time a short term realist.

With an e-reader you can control the size of the print.

In retirement when you can't think of something, it is when your brain farts.

Retirement is the reward for a job well done.

When you retire and move, things, like books, that had become invisible, become visible.

Approach the future with humility.

When climbing up and down the folding attic stairway, face the steps.

As a newlywed you want your husband home a lot, as the years pass by and he retires, you think, "What's he doing home now."

When you retire and interfere in your wife's routine, give her reasons to adjust to your retirement.

Not everyone feels privileged to hear the remarks of a "Dirty Old Man."

If you retire to a place where you can sit and see the sunrise and sunset, what do you do the remainder of the day?

You now travel with a suitcase for your medicine.

If sixty year old people spent as much effort trying to be a charming sixty year old instead of trying to be thirty, it sure would be nice.

You are more history than future.

The beginning of your life may never be clearer than at the end of your life.

You are never really gone until there is no one to remember you.

If you chose to wear a tie with your suit, then commit to button your top button.

You only need to wear your gym clothes to the gym.

Put your drink down when you have your photograph made.

When you attend a party, always have an exit strategy.

Sleep well.

If you discount anger, women are more emotional than men.

Rework your closet rather than following trends.

Mark your blue blazer inside with "blue" and your black blazer with "black," so you won't wear the black one thinking it is blue.

You look better with more clothes on, than off.

As you grow older, you always want a few young friends.

Drink very little liquid, if any, after 6 pm.

Driving at the speed limit is not a challenge.

In your younger days, your idiosyncrasy habits are rather irritating, but after age eighty they are considered cute.

You are the "Listener in Chief" or the "Resident Listener."

You hope your brain span matches your retirement life span.

Ballroom dancing twice a week reduces dementia.

After age fifty have a yearly comprehensive medical physical examination.

You don't have to hold in your stomach.

Ladies, dress your age: find the right look, lighter color hair softens the lines in your face, update your hairdo, and learn where to shop for your clothes.

It's hard to determine the difference between simple forgetfulness and a more serious memory loss.

Physical and mental activity along with a healthy diet can help you stay sharp.

If you walk into a room and can't remember what you came for, it's a good sign that you have awareness that you came into the room, not Alzheimer's Disease.

✦

Lose any weight and inches before retirement because after retirement it is hard to lose and when the weight comes off, it only comes off in your face.

✦

Think before you talk. You have not earned the right to say anything you want.

✦

You are not the center of attention.

✦

In retirement, it doesn't matter if you are "a big fish in a little pond" or a "little fish in a big pond," you are still a fish.

✦

Does it matter if you are hung with a new rope?

✦

Your eyesight won't get any worse.

✦

Your aching joints predict the weather.

✦

You can't estimate how long you will live.

✦

Be sure you don't overestimate how much you can withdraw from your savings and retirement accounts.

✦

Be neat and clean.

✦

Your grandchildren want quantity time rather than quality time.

✦

Why do you retain useless information but delete anything worth remembering.

✦

See if you can "test drive" a retirement home before you buy. In other words spend the night there.

Things don't replace relationships.

Try to never get out of shape.

The enemy of retirement isn't age, but inactivity.

Push hard, but not all the time.

You can't remember the secrets you are not supposed to tell.

You retire, life doesn't retire.

Stay active.

Vitamin D reduces risk for bone fracture.

Get fifteen minutes of sun every day.

Your physician doesn't ask you if you get up during the night to go to the bathroom, but how many times do you get up in the night.

Pick a financial adviser from a friend's recommendation, from your attorney's recommendation or your accountant's referral.

Clip coupons for the items you intend to stockpile.

Watch out for shrinking package sizes.

Rediscover your hidden talents and use them.

There is no such thing as the "empty-nest syndrome."

Concentrate on one hidden talent that gives you the most pleasure.

Take lessons.

Don't rush into retiring to a foreign country.

Buy a cell phone with large buttons, oversized text on the video screen, and a 20-decibel amplification.

A new test measuring proteins in the spinal fluid is eighty-seven percent accurate in predicting Alzheimer's Disease.

The new test for Alzheimer's Disease is ninety-five percent accurate in ruling out Alzheimer's Disease.

Cultivate curiosity.

The right haircut can take years off your looks.

Find and pursue your "next" and then your next "next."

Stay healthy on the inside.

Keep a good skin care routine.

Go with the flow.

See humor everywhere.

Serve your meals in courses to slow down eating so fast.

Assemble your own home gym with dumbbells, an inflatable fitness ball and a good pair of walking or running shoes.

When you retire you need to do something besides listening to your hearing aids.

Regardless of what the media says, don't let fear take over.

Remember that others are thinking: How long is it going to take you to get to your point?

With very little to occupy your time, consider whether the difficult situation is a flip or a catastrophe.

Money is not a prerequisite to live a happy retirement life, but it does provide security, confidence, and comfort.

Money is not one hundred percent of life, health and happiness is one percent.

Turn your passions into productive activities.

Enthusiasm on a big scale does equal passion and that passion takes you to exciting places.

A man wins his wife once before they marry, but a wife wants to be won every day, even in retirement.

Have your teeth bleached.

Your ears and nose grow larger, your lips thinner.

Retirement is sweeter if you love your spouse and put his/her interests above yours.

Just about everything comes to you when you are ready to receive it.

Retirement has its peak from which to view life.

Live today, it's the only day you truly have.

Experience only comes with time.

Tune out those who whisper your age in your ear.

What is the purpose of your life?

Don't make the mistake of doing nothing.

Begin your retirement, even if you start small.

There's still more to learn.

Your retired heart has no wrinkles.

As you use your body less, use your mind more.

Your accumulated hindsight gives you better insight and foresight.

The future contains much of the past.

The hardest of hearts can soften with kindness.

You are old if you add up your birthdays; young if you recognize your feelings.

Measure your age by attitude.

Often great persons distinguish themselves after age fifty.

When your husband retires and interferes in your routine, just get used to it.

Getting old is just giving up things.

You know you are old when you lean down to pick up something off the floor and while down you look for anything else on the floor to pick up.

There's nothing worse than an old man in an old Cadillac.

Still lead by example.

If your retired husband watches you mop and criticizes your method (after all these years), turn the job over to him permanently.

To win life's game depends on how you live the closing years.

Strive to be a pleasant person in your retirement.

Still put first things first.

You grew to here.

The mind and heart will solve most problems.

You still have a chance.

Age is in your mind.

Enjoy today.

A person in retirement must know how to get full value from all and everything.

There are no hard and fast rules for retirement because conditions vary.

There are pitfalls to retirement.

Retirement requires the basics of food, warmth, shelter and clothing. The rest is folly.

Luxuries may become unimportant.

You like that to which you have been accustomed.

✦

Retirement is survival.

✦

Do you pass up simplicity for want of luxuries?

✦

In retirement, your spouse's idiosyncrasies become magnified.

✦

Your heart and soul may be the only means of reaching safety in retirement.

✦

Why retire?

✦

Leave your spouse a note of your whereabouts when you leave the house for any length of time.

✦

How many puzzles can you work in retirement?

✦

In retirement you become lost not because of what you do, but because of what you leave undone.

✦

Your retirement map is in your mind.

✦

A natural "sense of direction" aids retirement.

✦

Do you retire to known surroundings or to a new location?

✦

In retirement if you lose your way, go back to the starting point.

✦

Distress signals are in threes: three flashes, three outbursts, three dots.

✦

If you stray from retirement and get "lost" the internal conflict of panic in the brain can be quite unnerving.

✦

To stay lost in retirement, you have to work at it.

✦

Retirement survival is just knowing where the dangers are, to recognize them and to use all the available resources.

Who influences your retirement?

What influences your retirement?

Weigh your unnecessary chances of possible loss against the possible gain.

Retirement requires a soft margin.

Don't let your spouse "suck the life out of you."

Survival in retirement depends on the individual.

What's it like to be alone in a room with your "dead" spouse?

Retirement is no more an option than to stop thinking.

Don't disengage from life.

Do you engineer your own downfall?

In retirement cultivate the vitality of intelligent conversation.

In retirement, do you feel "out of step" with everyone who is working?

How closely is your identity tied to your career?

Do you feel sorry for yourself?

In retirement if one spouse begins to complain, the other spouse must put a stop to it. It's like training for a marathon, but it can be done.

New structures for the day or the lack of structure.

Keep human contact.

Plug the leaks of wasteful spending.

Tear up the post office mailings offering scams and rip-offs.

Where is your will?

Comparison shop.

A walker and/or cane can cause serious falls.

Retirees are often marginalized. Everyone treats you like you are out of touch.

Your mental process is not as quick, but you are just as smart.

Can you multi-task?

Improve your communication skills.

Present yourself as physically alert and interesting.

Don't fold your arms across your chest so you won't appear judgmental.

Avoid starting conversations with negative words.

Start a conversation and get to the point quickly.

You try and then you die.

Live and learn, die and forget.

When you retire, it's okay to talk to yourself and answer yourself. But don't talk to yourself, answer yourself, and then say "huh."

Can you make decisions?

You won't know if you are senile, but others will know.

If you knew how long you were going to live, you could pro-rata out your money.

Learn the computer, answering services, and as many technological innovations as possible.

You know you are old when you go to bed tired and get up tired.

Retirement means you have the "license to reminisce."

In retirement there are never too many candles on your birthday cake.

To save money in retirement...with your manicure, don't put on polish, only buff your nails because your manicure will last longer.

The more you stay at home, the more you want to stay at home.

Will yourself to be happy.

When you retire, then inspire.

In retirement, optimism and health are connected.

In retirement, your organization is a higher level of empowerment.

Does retirement bring lists for each of your roles such as children, grandchildren, cleaning the home, and emergencies?

When you were a child, Christmas never got here. Now that you are old, it comes twice a year.

Happiness is a choice.

Quit believing in happy endings, but believe in good days.

Why don't women's clothes designers give more options. Not every retired woman can wear hip huggers.

Now that you are retired, you can get anything done if you write it down.

When you retire and your friends die and go to heaven, do you wonder if they are in the blue part or the white part of heaven.

When you are in your seventies and talk to your high school friends, you feel like you are a teenager, a gift.

There is no prescription for a positive attitude.

Optimists are predisposed to positive future expectations.

Pessimists think set-backs are unchangeable.

In retirement, is the glass half empty or half full?

Now that your hair is so thin, you don't have to sit as long under the hair dryer.

Keep your clothes clean from dirty spots and don't say, "Oh, no one will notice."

The second one hundred years are harder than the first one hundred years.

You will live longer if when driving, you make all right hand turns.

Wear colored shirts and blouses that have patterns and prints, so you won't notice the spilled food on them.

Life isn't easy, but worth the effort.

Try not to arrive at the airport more than six hours early for a flight.

Laugh often.

Like and love the ones who treat you right. Forget those who don't.

At the end of your retirement it seems like all your birthdays come at once.

Should you have given away all your hats?

If your days are limited you have to decide how to allocate your time.

The ultimate goal of retirement is to decide what is working and what isn't working.

Launch a new manifesto for slow communication. E-mail is too fast.

In retirement, how many joyful memories have been created in front of a television screen?

Death has been occurring consistently.

For Cleaners

For Cleaners
Or Housework That If Done Properly, Will Kill You

Have a clear plan.

Start at the back of the house and work to the front.

Vacuum draperies from top to the bottom.

Dust furnishings from the top of the room to the floor.

Use baskets to carry supplies.

Use "Dust-off" to clean electronic computer equipment.

When you locate them, keep important papers such as medical records and receipts in a file box.

Don't forget to clean the garage.

You can't have enough hooks to hang things.

Reward yourself for a job well done.

Everyone has junk drawers.

Get rid of expired foods.

Cracked dishes do no good.

Reorganize your kitchen as you clean.

Hire a professional cleaner.

Do you do what you do, not what you are told to do?

Why is housework not a profession?

Housewives can be hidden from history.

Housework is time consuming because it's never all done.

Be careful about combining cleaning agents. Some combinations are combustible.

Clean archival museum quality glass in frames with rubbing alcohol and a soft cloth.

To clean candle wax from a wood table: freeze with an ice cube and pop it off or soften with a hair dryer.

Keep your meat in the refrigerator in the plastic grocery bags to avoid any dripping.

Put each string of out of season Christmas lights in plastic grocery bags to store.

Pick up broken glass shards with a piece of bread.

Put a plastic bag in a vase and fill with water. When the flowers are dead remove the bag with flowers to avoid messy cleanup.

When your hands are messy in the kitchen and you need to answer the phone, slip a plastic bag on your hand.

Wash your hands between handling different foods such as meat and other foods such as vegetables.

Haul off raked leaves in the yard by making a tarp out of an old bed sheet.

When taking down your Christmas tree, lay your Christmas tree on a bed sheet to carry it outside.

Any cleaning solution containing petroleum distillates or petroleum hydrocarbons is flammable.

To clean a spot from fabric: place the fabric spot face down on an absorbent cloth, rub the spot gently from outward to inward with a cloth dampened with cleaning solvent, move the spot over the under blotting material. Dry and repeat if needed. Rinse or dry clean the piece.

Vinegar, baking soda and ammonia have stood the test of time.

Baking soda is a good grease cutter, less abrasive, and doesn't scratch surfaces.

Vinegar is a good cleaning agent.

Ammonia is a time tested cleaning agent.

Borax can be used when heavier scrubbing is needed.

Test each cleaning agent on the item before using.

To remove wax buildup on wood furniture: use one part vinegar to one part water, polish with equal parts of olive oil, denatured alcohol, gum turpentine and strained lemon juice, rub off excess and polish with another dry cloth.

Absorbent powders soak up moisture, grease and odors.

Talc and cornstarch soak up body moisture.

Fuller's earth removes grease from fabric and carpets.

Paste wax on furniture adds a patina that spray-on furniture polish does not.

Have you ever tried cheap vodka to clean a sink? It's antibacterial.

Baking soda absorbs unpleasant odors.

Deodorize carpets by sprinkling on baking soda, let stay a while, then vacuum.

Clean a reusable air conditioner filter by washing in detergent, rinse, dry and reinstall.

Disinfect a garbage can with Clorox Bleach.

To remove animal messes from the carpet: scoop up the mess, blot with paper towel, apply mixture of vinegar, lemon juice or ammonia. Scrub the area with soap and water.

Pour ammonia in your outside garbage bags and cans to deter any unwanted animals.

Clean brass and copper by first washing in warm soapy water, then clean with commercial cleaner or a paste of equal parts of salt, vinegar and flour.

Put a bobby pin or the teeth of a comb around a nail head to avoid hitting your finger with the hammer.

At the end of each day put all the cluttered items in one place as a "lost and found" department.

To remove indentations in carpet caused by furniture, put a damp bath towel on the spot, press with an iron.

To remove chewing gum from fabric: rub with a piece of ice wrapped in a plastic bag or put the item in the freezer to harden the gum, scrape with a dull edge tool.

To clear the room of cigarette odor: use a fan, a dish of ammonia or vinegar, or burn candles.

A drawer that doesn't glide easily can be remedied by rubbing the runners with soap or a candle.

To clean oil and grease from concrete garage floors: sprinkle cat litter on the spots, rub the litter with the bottom of your shoe, and sweep.

To clean your dishwasher, remove the spray arm, clear the ports with a pipe cleaner, scrub the filter screen, wipe down the tub and detergent dispenser, and if mineral deposits appear run the dishwasher through a cycle with a cup of vinegar in the detergent holder.

Take all the parts of a clothing ensemble to the dry cleaners because sometimes one item can fade slightly.

To dust spray the furniture polish onto a dry, clean cloth rather than pouring the polish directly onto the furniture.

Use a lamb's wool head instead of a feather duster. The wool absorbs the dust.

Spray a plastic container with Pam to avoid tomato stains.

Dry shampoo your hair by working a small amount of cornstarch into your hair and brush out with a dry, clean brush.

Use Q-tips to clean small places.

Clean a thermos bottle, glass decanter, glass vases and similar objects by putting in a denture tablet, let stand for a couple of hours, and rinse.

To remove sticky labels from glass, warm glass in microwave and afterwards use Goo-Gone.

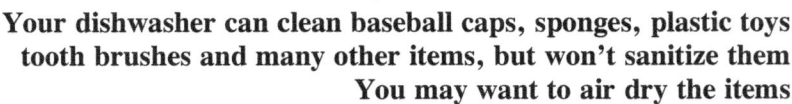

Let your children throw dice to see who has to do what chores. The high winner does the chore.

Your dishwasher can clean baseball caps, sponges, plastic toys, tooth brushes and many other items, but won't sanitize them. You may want to air dry the items.

When washing your automobile, to eliminate streaks add 1 Tablespoon of Jet-Dry to your car wash rinse.

A roach killer: three parts each of corn meal, sugar and boric acid. Put in jar lid tops or small dishes and place in safe places around the house, attic and basement.

White water spots on furniture may be lessened by rubbing with equal parts of non-gel toothpaste and baking soda.

To find a wall stud, run an electric razor over the wall and listen for the sound change.

Use an emery board to clean a dirty pencil eraser.

Fold and tape together two padded mailing envelopes to use as knee pads when kneeling.

Point an electric fan out a window to lessen odors from cooking foods that smell bad.

Mix a small amount of flour in your fertilizer distributor so when you spread it you can see where you missed.

Put clothes that have been sprinkled into the freezer just before ironing.

In hanging pictures, use chalk to mark the spot. It won't leave marks.

Before putting an item of clothing in the dirty clothes basket, attach a clothes pin to the area of clothes that need Spray and Wash.

Use an adhesive lint roller brush to remove cat and dog hair from upholstered furniture.

Dry the inside of your rubber gloves.

Rub your elbows with a lemon or grapefruit cut in half. The lemon cleans, the grapefruit exfoliates.

Use a hair dryer to hasten defrosting a freezer.

To avoid spills when adding water to the Christmas tree stand, add ice cubes instead of water.

Use an ID card to scrape spills off the top of a ceramic top stove.

Rub nails and screws with Chap Stick or soap to make them penetrate easily.

Wear loofah gloves dipped in a cleaning solution to clean the bath tubs.

To ward off wasps and bees on a picnic, put maple sugar or a sugary mixture on a piece of cardboard and place away from the picnic table to attract the bees and wasps.

Use four large binder clips to keep the plastic bag from slipping down inside the garbage can.

Place a paper plate beneath furniture legs to slide the piece more easily.

A housewife can't define her work outside of the family's well being.

A modern day cleaner spends all her time looking after the conveniences.

Freed from cleaning?

The manuals for housekeepers: cookbooks, women's magazines, and television.

Manuals tell information, not what the cleaner actually did.

Because women were the major housekeepers, in 1841 Catherine Beecher wrote *A Treastise on Domestic Economy for the Use of Young Ladies at Home and at School* which discussed the underestimated importance of women's roles in society.

Cleaning for money is a job different than cleaning for the family which is tied into other areas of the cleaner's life.

Homemaker's never retire.

There are no Fridays in a homemaker's life.

Plumbing and electricity made cleaning easier.

New technology such as electricity, washing machines, refrigeration, vacuum cleaners came in increments.

You don't carry water to the house anymore.

Wash the cleanest dishes first, then the greasy ones, and then the pots. Add hot water each time.

Dishwashers and clothes washing machines don't sort according to soil.

People used to wash on Monday, iron on Tuesday.

Having more water available leads to more washing clothes.

Your maid calls you: Miss, Mrs. or Mr.

How do you make cleaning a family adventure?

To clean a fiberglass tub and shower: use Spray and Wash with a tuffy-like sponge.

Get rid of expired prescriptions.

The top of picture frames conceals dust.

Replace used, dirty dish towels.

Outdoor barbecue grills need attention too.

Baseboards harbor dust.

Ceiling fan blades have a top side.

Dust and dirt is humbling.

Try not to whine.

Replace batteries in all battery operated equipment.

Be ruthless about throwing things away.

When it comes to getting rid of stuff, knowing how to get rid of it is essential: toss, reuse, sell, or recycle.

Video games are classic collectibles after twenty years.

Gadgets and technical products lose their value quickly.

Old Nordic-Track machines serve as clothes hangers in the bedroom.

A nickel or dime is a useful screwdriver.

Your first aid kit should be updated.

Window cleaner recipe: 1/2 cup white vinegar to 1 gallon of water.

To wash windows: 2-5 Tablespoons vinegar and 2 cups water with absorbent newspapers.

Your refrigerator and freezer needs cleaning from top to bottom, even the coils.

Ask for permission to put garage, yard or estate sale signs in the neighborhood, but remember to take them down.

Aim for a home free of dirt, grime and clutter.

To brighten pots: baking soda.

To clean bath and kitchen: 1 /2 cup Borax and 1 gallon water.

For scouring: sprinkle Borax, baking soda or salt on a damp sponge. Scour and rise.

To clean the oven: baking soda, salt and water.

To clean the toilet bowl: put a few Tablespoons baking soda in a bowl, then add 1 cup vinegar.

To clean the floor: vinegar in warm water.

A stronger version to clean floors: 4 Tablespoons of trisodium phosphate (from hardware store) to 1 gallon of hot water.

To open a drain: Pour in 1/2 cup baking soda, then 1 cup vinegar, plug drain until fizzing stops, then flush with hot water.

To clean the tile: equal amounts of vinegar and warm water.

Use a shower curtain with metal grommets.

Southpaws say "Hooray for left-handed scissors and commode handles."

Put five or six folded, used plastic grocery bags in the bottom of a small trash can for the next time, before lining with one used plastic grocery bag.

If your house is clean, just de-clutter it.

If your house is clean, vacuum after your overnight/week-end guest leaves.

Leave your bathroom vent on for ten minutes after you shower.

Remove the metal tab at the bottom of votive candles because it conducts heat.

When you make up a bed, a patterned bedspread is easier to line up the corners.

Cleaning the house is good exercise, mindless and brings a sense of accomplishment.

A modest degree of order is necessary for cleaning.

Use Borax and baking soda when you need to scrub a surface.

Set up a cleaning schedule that you follow as much as possible.

Set certain days, weeks or months to perform certain duties.

Determine jobs that need to be done every day and the time allowed for each such as making beds, washing dishes, reducing the clutter, garbage and bathrooms.

Determine jobs that need to be done once or twice a week and the time allowed for each such as vacuuming, dusting and watering plants.

Determine jobs that need to be done periodically and the time allowed such as woodwork, dusting picture frames, and closet cleaning.

Stock up on cleaning supplies by finding storage space that is easy to reach.

Can you share the cleaning work?

If one person undresses and dumps the clothes all over the room on the floor, put a "valet" chair nearby so all the clutter will be in one place.

If one person is neater than the other, negotiate an arrangement, but don't stand on principles.

Organize.

Jobs that need to be done.

De-clutter your home and/or office.

Does one cup of rainwater equal three gallons of city water?

You can't find good help anymore.

Keep the clutter in the kitchen to a minimum.

If trying to straighten up a toddler's room full of toy parts, just use a yard rake.

Rub china cups with salt to remove coffee or tea stains.

Sprinkle salt or baking soda on a plate with dried egg residue.

Clean diamond jewelry in a solution of three parts of water, ammonia, and detergent.

To clean real pearls, wear them against your skin.

Lamp shades can be cleaned with a soft brush or lamb's wool duster. Dust inside and outside.

Clean spots on a paper lamp shade with an art-gum eraser.

Remove the cellophane from the lamp shade because it may shrink from the light bulb heat, distort the frame, and put scorched marks on the inside of the lampshade.

In hanging picture frames, the longer the leveler the more accurate it is.

Wash plastic shower curtains in the washing machine.

Silverfish don't like to be disturbed, so vacuum often. Apply a two percent diazinon dust to areas that are safe from pets and humans.

To protect the floor from an artist's acrylic, oil or watercolor spills, place a used plastic shower curtain under an artist's easel.

When you have emptied the foaming anti-bacterial gel bottle, then add diluted liquid Dial soap for another foaming bottle.

To repair a torn shower curtain hole, put heavy adhesive tape on either side of the hole. Then punch a hole in the shower curtain with a hole punch.

When washing towels in the washing machine, don't add fabric softener or dryer sheets because it inhibits the cotton's natural absorbency.

Use a used toothbrush or an old electric toothbrush to clean tub grout.

For Emergency Preparers

For Emergency Preparers

Or Emergency Preparedness and For Staying at Home After the Electricity Goes Off

Each emergency whether natural or man-made will require different disaster plans for the family, each individual, and with each member having responsibilities. Some types of disasters are tornado, hurricane, earthquake, fire, severe weather, and terrorist attack.

Emergency Preparedness

Get ready to fumble in the dark.

Two year old canned peas taste better than you think.

Privacy in a dark bedroom means everyone's windows are open.

Starbucks coffee is off limits.

Huddle around a battery powered weather radio.

You can eat peanut butter and jelly for three meals a day.

The eleven hour nights indicate that Tylenol PM is okay.

A friend with a chain saw is your best friend.

Ice is a bartering item.

Lines for gasoline are the norm.

Barbecue everything that is in the freezer.

Hair does dry without a blow dryer.

Baseball caps are acceptable with any outfit.

Fruit tastes better in the dark.

How do you train yourself not to flip on the light switch when you enter a room.

Contact your neighbors.

A ham radio operator keeps you posted when the television and radio are not working.

No electricity does clean out the refrigerator and freezer.

Garage doors can be opened manually.

When the lights come on, shut the windows. The air conditioning is on.

Do you have surge protectors?

Hunker down.

You are not alone in the neighborhood.

Plan an evacuation route.

NOAA is the National Oceanic and Atmosphere Administration.

The following lists overlap according to whether you are staying at home or evacuating.

For Staying at Home

Designate an inside room that hopefully won't be hit by a falling tree.

Make a "nest" in the designated area.

Avoid rooms with glass windows.

Don't open windows if tornados are predicted.

Board up windows.

Secure all loose items outside.

Stock your pantry.

It is suggested that you have at least three days of supplies.

Try to have one gallon of water per person per day.

If you have electricity you can freeze water to drink later as it melts.

Unscented liquid household bleach for water purification.

If the electricity is damaged, stock plenty of ice.

Keep two ice chests, one for ice, one for food storage.

Frozen gel packs are handy to replace ice.

Keep matches dry.

Have rain gear handy.

Wear rubber boots in case of flooding.

Use your cell phone and charger for as long as you have electricity. If you have a NOAA radio, it has a cell phone charger.

Put the letters ICE in cell telephone with name of person/persons to contact "in case of emergency."

Use land line telephone until the telephone and/or electricity is not working.

Have a compass if you leave the house.

Keep a recent picture of family members and pets in waterproof sleeve.

Keep favorite game or toy for children.

Put name on each person.

Keep flashlights and batteries.

Battery operated fluorescent lights are very efficient.

Have a battery operated radio, preferably with an NOAA channel and an outlet for recharging the battery and cell telephone.

Radio disk jockeys keep information flowing during emergency.

Keep car full of gasoline at all times. Fill up generators, extra gas canisters, four-wheelers. For generators you can siphon gasoline from your car.

Use swimming pool water to flush toilets if sewer line is damaged.

Fill bathtubs with water to flush toilets.

Generators:

Place outside the house and away from doors, windows and vents.

Keep generator dry.

Place carbon monoxide detector in your home.

Be sure to cut off electric line to the house before using.

Run 5-6 hours at a time only outside in ventilated area.

Connect to essentials: refrigerator, freezer, fan, electric heater, and not the air conditioner.

Use 10-12 gauge heavy duty extension cords.

Be careful, if you feel dizzy or weak. Get fresh air immediately.

Use clear, water tight plastic containers and place off the floor in case of flooding.

Unplug appliances and electronics.

Keep fire extinguisher in a convenient place and know how to use it.

First Aid Kit:

sterile gloves

sterile gauze

soap

antibiotic ointment–Neosporin

handi-wipes

burn ointment

thermometer

Band-aids

Keep cash and credit cards.

Have prescriptions, medicines and copy of prescriptions.

In a waterproof container or bag, place family documents such as: bank account numbers, birth, marriage certificates, insurance policies and any other valuable papers.

Have personal hygiene materials.

Keep a supply of canned and non-perishable foods (not requiring refrigeration) such as chicken, tuna, salmon, potato chips, peanut butter, nuts, dried fruits, and protein bars.

Use a manual can opener.

Use Sterno cooking equipment.

Keep a supply of plastic knives, forks, spoons, and serving knife, spoon and fork.

Have a utility knife.

Use work gloves.

Use paper plates, plastic cups, paper napkins and paper towels.

Have phone numbers for family, friends and physicians.

Have extra prescription glasses or hearing aids with batteries.

Keep a supply of nose and mouth protection masks with a N95 rating to filter-out ninety-five percent of particles 0.3 microns or larger.

Plastic sheets to protect yourself if roof blown off.

Keep a supply of duct tape nearby.

A good supply of toilet paper is useful.

Baby wipes can be used for bathing if water not available.

Use a whistle to alert anyone.

Use a shovel to dig out debris.

Keep basic tools such as hammer, pliers, and screwdriver.

Have a change of clothing and footwear.

Have a good supply of plastic bags for waste.

Have items for debris clean-up.

Avoid "rubbernecking" so clean-up crews can work.

Only go to the hospital emergency room for life-threatening situations.

For babies:

Baby food and formula

Diapers

Powdered milk

Baby wipes

Medicines

Diaper rash ointment

Plastic bags for waste.

A Family Plan

Know how to escape from each room of the house as well as from the neighborhood.

There should be two exits from each room. Supply hammers or tools to break open windows.

Know how to contact family members in case of separation.

Designate an out-of-state person whom everyone can call.

Know emergency personnel numbers and keep your telephone book handy.

Know how to disconnect home utilities such as gas, water and electricity in case of gas leak or fire.

Keep a shut off wrench or necessary tool near these utilities to shut off.

If you shut off gas, you need a professional to turn it back on.

Keep copies of valuable personal papers at a safe, remote location.

Know the extra steps to take for special needs of the young, old, or physically challenged.

Know how to perform CPR and first aid.

Have a plan for any pets.

Teach children to dial and talk to 911.

Post emergency telephone numbers (fire, ambulance, police, medical services) by all telephones and on cell phones.

Familiarize yourself and others with fire extinguishers:

PASS:

Pull the pin.
Aim at the base of the flames.
Squeeze the trigger.
Sweep back and forth along the flames.

Install smoke and carbon monoxide detectors on every level of your home, in all bedrooms, in all common halls and outside of sleeping areas.

Consider installing new interconnected wireless smoke detectors. When one goes off, all go off.

Have identification on each person and any individual medical needs.

For Neighborhoods

Rally neighbors to work together.

Share generators and medical skills.

Be sure children are cared for if parents not able to get home.

Identify elderly and their needs.

Eat with neighbors who can provide a meal, then another house the next night. Cook the most perishable food first.

Cook on gas or charcoal grill outside.

Check with schools for their plans to care for children and how they will communicate with parents if children unable to get home. Be sure the schools have water, food, basic supplies, and assigned shelter.

Check the ventilation system at workplace to filter contaminants, know how to turn off gas and other utilities. Stock up on appropriate supplies such as water, food, and first aid.

To Evacuate

Put a small emergency kit in trunk of car.

Adopt an evacuation route.

Be prepared for "bumper-to-bumper" traffic.

Evacuate by designated zones; the people living nearest the shoreline evacuate first.

If you come upon a flooded road, turn back.

Take detailed road maps and be familiar with alternate routes.

Plan for motels, hotels, and places to stop along the way.

If you don't have a car, plan how to evacuate.

Keep automobile gasoline tank full at all times.

Extra gasoline can be bought before the emergency.

If time allows, e-mail or call out-of-state contact or leave a note telling where you are going.

Take plastic bags for waste.

Take sleeping material such as blankets, sleeping bags, pillows, tent, and extra clothes.

Have personal hygiene items such as tooth paste, comb and brush, feminine hygiene products and special supplies for dentures, contact lenses, and hearing aids.

Supply equipment for any special needs person.

Be sure to have cash and/or credit cards.

Take extra set of car keys and house keys.

Paper, pencils, and notepads are useful.

Be sure you have identification on your body.

Take food for any pets, pop-up travel water bowl, leash and information on hotels that take pets.

Consult list "For Staying at Home."

For a Chemical Attack

Create a safe room such as an interior room with no windows or just one window.

Seal any doors or windows with duct tape.

Place wet towel under door.

Turn off air conditioning unit and vents.

Assembly any needed items as listed above.

Stay inside uncontaminated room until given the "all clear" sign.

As you exit cover nose and mouth with wet cloth.

Types of Hurricanes

Category 1 (74-95 mph): Damage primarily to unanchored mobile homes, shrubbery, and trees. Some coastal road flooding and minor pier damage.

Category 2 (96-110 mph): Some damage to roofs, doors, windows, trees and shrubbery. Pier flooding.

Category 3 (111-130 mph): Some structural damage; large trees downed; flooding near shoreline and possibly inland; mobile homes destroyed.

Category 4 (131-155 mph): Extensive damage to doors and windows; major damage to lower floors near shore; terrain may be flooded inland.

Category 5 (over 155 mph): Complete roof failure; some building failures; massive evacuation; major flooding damage to lower floors of all shoreline buildings.

www.ingramcontent.com/pod-product-compliance
Lightning Source LLC
Chambersburg PA
CBHW020050170426
43199CB00009B/228
9781632932969